Wanda E. Brunstetter's

Amish
Friends
COOKBOOK

200 Hearty Recipes from Amish Country

Wanda E. Brunstetter's

Amish
Friends
COOKBOOK

200 Hearty Recipes from Amish Country

BARBOUR
PUBLISHING

ISBN 978-1-59789-644-3

Cover art and interior photos by Doyle Yoder Photography
Cover and interior design by Robyn Martins

Published by Barbour Publishing, Inc., P.O. Box 719, Uhrichsville, Ohio 44683, www.barbourbooks.com

Our mission is to publish and distribute inspirational products offering exceptional value and biblical encouragement to the masses.

Member of the
Evangelical Christian
Publishers Association

Printed in China.

Dedication

To all of my special Amish and Mennonite friends.

Acknowledgments

I would like to thank the following people for their help with typing, sorting, proofing, and taste testing so this recipe book could be put together: Donna Crow, Vern Barnes, Jean Brunstetter, Lorine VanCorbach, and Richard Brunstetter. Thanks also goes to all of the Amish and Mennonite women who willingly shared their recipes with me, as well as to Kelly Williams and Rebecca Germany, my helpful editors, and everyone else at Barbour Publishing who made this project possible.

Contents

History of the Amish and Mennonites

The Amish and Mennonites are direct descendants of the Anabaptists, a group that emerged from the Reformation in Switzerland in 1525 and developed separately in Holland a few years later. Most Anabaptists eventually became identified as Mennonites, after a prominent Dutch leader, Menno Simons. The word *Amish* comes from Jacob Ammann, an influential leader who in 1693 led a group that separated from the Mennonite churches. Driven by persecution from their homes in Switzerland and Germany, hundreds of Mennonites began to immigrate to North America, and in the 1700s the Amish sought homes in North America, too. They were welcomed in Pennsylvania by William Penn and first settled there by the mid-nineteenth century. Some moved to Ohio, Indiana, Iowa, and other parts of the country. Both the Amish and Mennonites believe in the authority of the Scriptures, and their willingness to stand apart from the rest of the world shows through their simple, plain way of living.

Beverages

Whether therefore ye eat, or drink,
or whatsoever ye do,
do all to the glory of God.
1 CORINTHIANS 10:31

Quick Root Beer

1 teaspoon yeast
1½ cups sugar
4 teaspoons root beer extract
Warm water

In 1-gallon jar, dissolve yeast in 1 cup warm water. Add sugar and root beer extract with enough warm water to dissolve thoroughly. Stir until dissolved. Fill jar with water and set in the sun or a warm place for several hours or until strong enough. Cool. Note: Root beer can be made in the morning and be ready to drink by noon.

Susie Martin
Penn Yan, NY

Good, better, best—never let let it rest.

Cappuccino Mix

1 cup instant creamer
1 cup chocolate drink mix
⅔ cup instant coffee granules
½ cup sugar
½ teaspoon cinnamon
¼ teaspoon nutmeg

Combine all ingredients and store in airtight container. To prepare, add 3 tablespoons mix to 6 ounces hot water or milk. Stir well.

Martha Weaver
Mertztown, PA

The teakettle sings even when it's up to its neck in hot water.

Effortless Eggnog

½ gallon cold milk, divided
1 (3.4 ounce) package French vanilla instant
   pudding mix
¼ cup sugar
2 teaspoons vanilla
½ teaspoon cinnamon
½ teaspoon nutmeg

In large bowl, whisk ¾ cup milk and pudding mix until smooth. Whisk in sugar, vanilla, cinnamon, and nutmeg. Stir in remaining milk. Refrigerate until serving. Yields 2 quarts.

Rosella Oberholtzer
Mifflinburg, PA

Hay-Time Switchel

2 cups sugar
1 cup molasses
¼ cup vinegar
1 teaspoon ginger
1 gallon water, divided

Heat sugar, molasses, vinegar, and ginger in 1 quart water until dissolved. Add remaining water; chill and serve. Yields 1 gallon.

Mollie Stoltzfus
Charlotte Hall, MD

If you can't be thankful for what you receive, then be thankful for what you escape.

Homemade Vegetable Juice

I gallon tomatoes
3 quarts carrots
2 quarts red beets
I quart celery
6 onions
Handful of parsley
Juice from I to 2 lemons
Salt
3 to 4 hot peppers (optional)

In large kettle, boil vegetables and parsley for I hour until soft. Put through food mill or blender. Add lemon juice and salt. Pour into jars and seal. Process jars in boiling water bath for 10 minutes.

Lena Miller
Apple Creek, OH

Fruit Slush

I (6 ounce) can frozen orange juice concentrate,
   thawed
3 cups water
I½ cups sugar
6 bananas, mashed
I (20 ounce) can crushed pineapple, drained
7UP (optional)

Mix concentrate, water, and sugar. Add bananas and pineapple and stir. Freeze. To serve, thaw to slush. Add 7UP if desired.

Ruth Troyer
Orwell, OH

Cheery Cherry Punch

3 (3 ounce) packages cherry gelatin
2 cups sugar
6 cups boiling water
1 (46 ounce) can unsweetened pineapple juice
1 (12 ounce) can frozen orange juice concentrate,
   thawed
1 (12 ounce) can frozen lemonade concentrate,
   thawed
1 gallon cold water
2 (2 liter) bottles ginger ale

Dissolve gelatin and sugar in boiling water. Add pineapple juice, orange juice and lemonade concentrates, and water. Mix well. Chill until very cold. Just before serving, add ginger ale and ice.

Linda Fisher
Leola, PA

Grape Punch

1 (6 ounce) can frozen white grape
   juice concentrate, thawed
4 cups water
1 (2 liter) bottle 7UP
½ gallon raspberry sherbet

Mix all ingredients together. Add 7UP and sherbet last.

Ina Mast
West Union, OH

• • •

*A cookbook is a volume
full of stirring
passages.*

• • •

Vinegar Punch

2 quarts water
¼ cup vinegar
½ cup sugar
⅛ teaspoon nutmeg

In large pitcher, measure water. Add vinegar, sugar, and nutmeg. Stir until sugar is dissolved.

Ruth Martin
Selinsgrove, PA

Rhubarb Punch

12 cups chopped rhubarb
8 cups water
3 cups sugar
1 (12 ounce) can frozen orange juice concentrate, thawed

Cook rhubarb in water until done. Let drip through sieve, collecting juice in large container. Add sugar, orange juice concentrate, and water to equal 3 gallons.

Elva Shirk
Dundee, NY

Amish Church

Amish church services are held every other Sunday in Amish homes. Mennonites worship in a separate meetinghouse. The geographic area where the Amish live is divided into church districts, and each family normally hosts church about once a year. As people arrive, the buggies are parked and the horses are put inside the barn or in a corral.

Church begins around 8:00 a.m. The women and girls are seated in one area, while the men and boys occupy another. Seating is on backless wooden benches, which each district owns and transports from house to house in a bench wagon.

The three-hour service begins with the congregation singing from the *Ausbund* (Amish church hymnal). During this time, the church leaders meet in a separate room to decide who will preach the two sermons that day. The first sermon usually begins around 8:30 a.m. and last about thirty minutes. Scriptures are read then, and the congregation kneels for silent prayer. Next, the main sermon is preached, often lasting as long as one hour. When the main sermon is over, the other ministers usually make short statements that emphasize what has been said. The congregation takes part in another half hour of prayer and singing before the service concludes.

Following church, a simple meal is served, usually consisting of sandwiches made with Amish peanut butter. The meal also might include apple butter, red beets, pickles, cheese, and cookies. A silent prayer is offered before and after the meal, and a time of fellowship follows.

Bread and Rolls

*Cast thy bread upon the waters: for thou
shalt find it after many days.*

ECCLESIASTES 11:1

Grandma's Honey Wheat Bread

4 cups warm water

2 heaping tablespoons yeast

1 egg

¾ cup vegetable oil

½ cup honey

½ cup wheat germ

1 tablespoon salt

2 cups whole-wheat flour

9 cups all-purpose flour (approximately)

Preheat oven to 350°. Whisk together first seven ingredients. Add wheat flour first and up to 9 cups all-purpose flour. Let rise until double. Punch down and shape into loaves. Let rise to double again. Bake for 50 to 60 minutes. Yields 4 large loaves or 5 small ones.

Emma Raber
Holmesville, OH

Ask God to bless your food, but don't expect Him to make your bread.

Baked Doughnuts

2 heaping tablespoons yeast
2½ cups warm water
2 eggs
¾ cup sugar
¾ cup butter, softened
2½ teaspoons salt
4 cups flour
1 (21 ounce) can pie filling (any flavor)

Preheat oven to 350°. Dissolve yeast in warm water. In separate bowl, beat eggs, sugar, butter, and salt. Stir in yeast and 4 cups flour (more if needed). Don't overmix. (Dough will be sticky.) Transfer dough to another bowl, cover tightly, and refrigerate overnight. The next day, roll out dough with plenty of flour. Cut with doughnut cutter (no hole). Place doughnuts on cookie sheets and let rise. Indent centers of doughnuts with finger and fill with pie filling. Bake for 8 to 10 minutes or until light brown. Cool and drizzle with icing.

Icing
½ cup butter, softened
3⅓ cups powdered sugar
1 teaspoon vanilla
6 tablespoons milk

Beat icing ingredients until smooth.

Mrs. Mervin Hoover
Curtiss, WI

Green Pepper and Cheddar Corn Bread

1 cup finely chopped green pepper
½ cup chopped onion
3 tablespoons butter
1 cup yellow cornmeal
½ teaspoon salt
1 cup plain yogurt
4 teaspoons double-acting baking powder
½ cup butter, melted
2 eggs, well beaten
¼ pound sharp cheddar cheese, very finely diced

Preheat oven to 350°. Cook green pepper and onion in 3 tablespoons butter on medium heat until tender, about 10 minutes, stirring occasionally. Transfer to mixing bowl and add remaining ingredients. Mix just until moistened. Pour into well-buttered 8-inch square baking dish. Bake for 25 to 30 minutes or until toothpick inserted in center comes out clean. Serve very hot.

Mollie Stoltzfus
Charlotte Hall, MD

Oatmeal
Bread

4 cups boiling water

2 cups quick oats

1 cup whole-wheat flour

½ cup brown sugar or honey

4 tablespoons butter

2 tablespoons salt

2 tablespoons yeast

1 cup warm water

¼ cup vinegar

12 to 14 cups all-purpose flour

Preheat oven to 350°. Pour boiling water over oats, whole-wheat flour, sugar, butter, and salt; mix well. Cool until lukewarm. Dissolve yeast in 1 cup warm water. Mix into batter along with vinegar and all-purpose flour. Set in warm place and let rise until doubled. Punch down and shape into four loaves. Bake for 30 minutes or until done.

Mrs. Henry Leid
Elkton, KY

Easy Dinner Rolls

2 packages dry yeast
¾ cup warm water
⅓ cup sugar
I teaspoon salt
I egg, beaten
½ cup butter, melted
3 to 3½ cups flour, divided

Preheat oven to 375°. Dissolve yeast in warm water. Add sugar, salt, egg, butter, and I cup flour; mix well. Stir in enough flour to make a soft dough; mix well. Shape dough into ball. Grease dough, turning to grease all sides. Return dough to bowl. Cover; let rise until doubled. Punch down and shape into balls; let rise for 30 minutes or longer. Bake for 8 to 12 minutes. Yields about 12 rolls.

Mary Hoover
Fortuna, MO

◆ ◆ ◆

If you are waiting for
something to turn up,
try your sleeves.

◆ ◆ ◆

Banana Bran Muffins

1 cup flour
1 cup oat bran
1 teaspoon baking soda
½ teaspoon salt
½ cup chopped walnuts or pecans
1 cup mashed ripe bananas (2 large)
½ cup butter
½ cup brown sugar
1 egg

Preheat oven to 375°. In medium bowl, stir together flour, oat bran, baking soda, salt, and nuts. In separate bowl, beat bananas and butter. Add brown sugar and egg; beat until completely mixed. Add dry ingredients and stir just until blended. Spoon into greased muffin tins, filling each about three-quarters full. Bake for 15 to 20 minutes or until toothpick inserted in center of muffin comes out clean. Let cool in tins for 5 minutes before removing. Yields about one dozen.

Norma Zimmerman
Latham, MO

Sweet Potato
Biscuits

1 cup flour
2 teaspoons baking powder
1 teaspoon salt
½ cup sugar
1 cup mashed sweet potatoes
3 tablespoons shortening
⅓ cup milk

Preheat oven to 400°. Mix all ingredients together. Roll out dough on floured board and cut with cutter. Bake on greased cookie sheets for 20 minutes. Yields one dozen.

Lorraine Brubacher
Leonardtown, MD

*The secret of success
is to start from scratch
and then keep on scratching.*

Pumpkin Bran Muffins

4 eggs

2 cups sugar

1½ cups vegetable oil

2 teaspoons baking powder

2 teaspoons baking soda

1 teaspoon salt

1 teaspoon cinnamon

2 cups mashed cooked pumpkin

3 cups bran

2 cups flour

1 cup raisins

Preheat oven to 350°. In large bowl, beat eggs; add sugar, oil, baking powder, baking soda, salt, cinnamon, and pumpkin. Beat well. Add bran, flour, and raisins. Stir until well blended. Spoon into greased muffin tins and bake for 20 minutes. Yields 2½ dozen.

Lena Martin
Trenton, KY

Bacon 'n' Cheese Muffins

½ pound bacon

Vegetable oil

1 egg, beaten

¾ cup milk

1¾ cups flour

¼ cup sugar

1 tablespoon baking powder

½ cup cornflakes

1 cup shredded cheese

Preheat oven to 400°. Fry bacon and reserve drippings. If necessary, add vegetable oil to drippings to make ⅓ cup. In medium bowl, combine drippings, egg, and milk; set aside. In separate bowl, combine flour, sugar, and baking powder; add to drippings mixture and stir until moistened. Fold in crumbled bacon, cornflakes, and shredded cheese. Spoon into greased muffin tins and bake for 15 to 20 minutes. Yields about 1 dozen.

Ada Miller
Norwalk, WI

Pineapple Zucchini Bread

3 eggs, beaten
2 cups finely shredded zucchini
1 cup vegetable oil
1 (8 ounce) can crushed
  pineapple, drained
2 teaspoons vanilla
3 cups flour
2 cups sugar

½ teaspoon baking powder
2 teaspoons baking soda
1 teaspoon salt
1½ teaspoons cinamon
¾ teaspoon nutmeg
1 cup chopped nuts
1 cup chocolate chips or raisins

Preheat oven to 350°. In mixing bowl, combine eggs, zucchini, oil, pineapple, and vanilla. Combine dry ingredients and stir into egg mixture just until moistened. Fold in nuts and chocolate chips or raisins. Pour into two greased 4x8-inch loaf pans. Bake for 50 to 60 minutes or until toothpick inserted in center comes out clean. Cool before removing from pans to wire racks.

Ruth Weaver
Millersburg, OH

*Worry is
interest paid on
trouble before it is due.*

Morning Glory Muffins

4 eggs

1⅓ cups vegetable oil

1 teaspoon vanilla

3 cups flour

1¼ cups brown sugar

3 teaspoons baking soda

¾ teaspoon salt

3 teaspoons cinnamon

3 cups shredded carrots

¾ cup flaked coconut

1 large apple, shredded

⅓ cup nuts

½ cup raisins

Preheat oven to 350°. In mixing bowl, beat eggs, oil, and vanilla. Combine remaining ingredients and stir into egg mixture just until moistened. Spoon into greased muffin tins and bake for 15 to 20 minutes. Yields 2½ dozen muffins.

Dorothy Glick
Augusta, WV

Unleavened Bread
(for Communion)

1½ cups flour
¼ teaspoon salt
¼ cup shortening
⅓ to ½ cup milk

Preheat oven to 400°. Mix flour, salt, and shortening with pastry cutter. Add enough milk to make a wet dough. Form dough into two balls. Roll out one ball of dough to about ⅛-inch thickness. Prick with fork. With two pancake turners, transfer dough to slightly greased cookie sheet. Roll out second ball and repeat process. Cut into squares with cutter and bake for 8 minutes. Yields about 100 pieces. Note: Do not double recipe. Make a single recipe at a time.

Mary Schwartz
Nottawa, MI

◆ ◆ ◆

*Troubled waters cleanse
the garments best.*

◆ ◆ ◆

𝒮Amish Schools

Amish children begin school in the first grade and end their schooling after eighth grade, at which time they learn some kind of trade. Although some Amish children attend public schools, most are taught in their own one-room schoolhouses. Normally just one teacher oversees all eight grades, but most teachers do have a helper, and some larger schools have two or three teachers.

A typical school day begins with a period of devotions, as a passage of scripture is read from the Bible. Following Bible reading, the children repeat the Lord's Prayer in unison. Next, they sing a few songs. Arithmetic is the first subject of the day; then comes spelling or English. Since German-speaking Amish children are taught the English language in the first grade, the teacher must give attention to them while the other children work on their own or with the assistance of the teacher's helper.

Amish parents are involved with the school in several ways. They not only take responsibility for being on the school board and hiring the teachers, but also do the repairs and annual cleaning of the schoolhouses a few weeks before school begins each term. Most parents visit the school once or twice during the year, often dropping by without prior notice. Sometimes a hot lunch is brought to school by a parent, and various school programs are always well attended by the children's parents.

Breakfast Foods

The LORD is my portion,
saith my soul;
therefore will I hope in him.
LAMENTATIONS 3:24

Overnight Caramel French Toast

1 cup brown sugar
½ cup butter
2 tablespoons light corn syrup
12 slices bread
¼ cup sugar
1 teaspoon cinnamon, divided
6 eggs
1½ cups milk
1 teaspoon vanilla

In saucepan on medium heat, bring brown sugar, butter, and light corn syrup to a boil. Pour into greased 9x13-inch baking dish. Top with 6 bread slices. Combine sugar and ½ teaspoon cinnamon and sprinkle half over bread. Place remaining bread on top and sprinkle with remaining cinnamon-sugar mixture. In large bowl, beat eggs, milk, vanilla, and remaining ½ teaspoon cinnamon. Pour over bread. Refrigerate overnight. The next morning, preheat oven to 350° and bake for 30 to 35 minutes.

Barbara King
Paradise, PA

Breakfast Fried Zucchini

4 cups shredded zucchini
½ teaspoon salt
½ cup milk
2 eggs, beaten
1 cup cracker crumbs

Fry salted zucchini in skillet until soft. Combine milk, eggs, and cracker crumbs; add to cooked zucchini. Fry until firm. Add ground beef or bacon pieces if desired.

Mary Zimmerman
Mifflinburg, PA

Hidden Eggs

Bread
4 tablespoons butter, melted and divided
6 eggs
Salt and pepper to taste
I to 2 cups shredded cheddar cheese

Preheat oven to 350°. In 9-inch square pan, break up enough bread to cover bottom of pan and drizzle with 2 tablespoons melted butter. Break eggs over bread and sprinkle with salt and pepper. Break up more bread and spread on top of eggs. Drizzle with remaining 2 tablespoons butter and top with shredded cheese. Bake for 15 to 20 minutes or until eggs are done.

Linda Fisher
Leola, PA

A good disposition is worth more than gold.

Farmer's Breakfast

½ pound bacon
1 onion, chopped
3 cooked potatoes, cubed or shredded
5 eggs
Salt and pepper to taste
1 cup shredded cheddar cheese
Chopped fresh parsley

Cook bacon and onions in skillet until bacon is crisp. Remove bacon from skillet. Drain all but ½ cup drippings. Add potatoes and brown. Return bacon and onions to skillet. Make five wells in potatoes and break one egg into each. Season with salt and pepper; sprinkle with cheese. Cover and cook on low heat for 5 to 10 minutes or until eggs are set. Garnish with parsley. Serve immediately.

Katie Zook
Apple Creek, OH

Baked Oatmeal

2 eggs
I cup sugar
½ cup butter or margarine, melted
3 cups oatmeal
I cup milk
2 teaspoons baking powder
Pinch of salt

Preheat oven to 350°. Combine eggs, sugar, and butter in 2-quart baking dish. Add oatmeal, milk, baking powder, and salt; stir until well blended. Bake for 30 minutes. Add milk or scoop of ice cream.

Barbara King
Paradise, PA

Success in marriage isn't finding the right person; it's being the right person.

Yoder's Pancakes

5 cups flour
5 heaping teaspoons baking powder
1 teaspoon salt
1 cup vegetable oil
2 eggs
4 cups milk

In 4-quart mixing bowl, measure flour, baking powder, and salt. Mix well. Make well in center and fill with oil, eggs, and 2 cups milk; beat well with a spoon. Fold in remaining milk while scraping sides of bowl. Stir just until blended; batter should be lumpy. Ladle 3 tablespoons batter into hot, greased skillet. When bubbly around edges, flip over. Flip several times until well done. Yields about 18 large pancakes.

Mary Yoder
Waldron, MI

Fluffy Pumpkin Pancakes

2 cups flour
4 teaspoons baking powder
1 teaspoon salt
2 tablespoons sugar
2 cups milk
1 tablespoon butter, melted
1 cup mashed pumpkin
2 eggs, separated

In large bowl, sift dry ingredients. In blender, mix milk, butter, pumpkin, and egg yolks. Stir into dry ingredients. Beat egg whites until stiff and fold in at last. Ladle into hot greased skillet. When bubbly around edges, flip over. Cook until done.

Mrs. Mervin Hoover
Curtiss, WI

Sausage Breakfast Casserole

6 slices bread
¼ to ½ cup butter
1½ pounds sausage
1½ cups shredded cheddar cheese
6 eggs
3 cups milk
1 teaspoon salt

Spread butter on bread. Arrange in greased 9x13-inch baking dish. Brown sausage and drain well in colander. Spoon over bread slices and sprinkle with cheese. Combine eggs, milk, and salt; mix well. Pour over cheese and refrigerate overnight. The next morning, preheat oven to 350°. Bake for 45 minutes or until set. Add Tater Tots or shredded potatoes on top if desired.

Mrs. Joe Schwartz
Geneva, IN

◆ ◆ ◆

Kindness is the oil that takes the friction out of life.

◆ ◆ ◆

Granola Cereal

4 cups rolled oats
8 cups oatmeal
1 cup wheat germ
1 cup flaked coconut
½ cup sunflower seeds
1 cup pecans
1 cup brown sugar
1 teaspoon cinnamon
½ teaspoon salt
1 cup butter, melted
1 cup honey (melt with butter)

Preheat oven to 325°. Mix all ingredients together and spread in shallow baking pan. Bake for 30 minutes or until lightly browned, stirring every 15 minutes.

Linda Esh
Paradise, PA

Good
Grape Nuts

7 cups whole-wheat flour

3 cups brown sugar

4 cups soured milk or buttermilk

2 teaspoons baking soda

2 teaspoons salt

½ cup margarine, melted

2 teaspoons vanilla

Preheat oven to 250°. Mix all ingredients together and spread in shallow baking pan. Bake for 1½ to 2 hours. When cool, crumble and toast in a 250° oven for 30 minutes. Store in plastic bags when cool.

Florence Schwartz
Livingston, WI

Amish Weddings

The Amish wedding season often occurs in the fall, after the harvest is completed. However, in some areas, Amish weddings are held at other times throughout the year. The bride and groom both have two attendants, called *Newehockers* or *Newesitzers* (side sitters). Other helpers include the *Forgeher* (ushers), the waiters who serve tables during the meal afterward, the cooks, the helpers who set up tables, and the *Hostlers* (the boys who take care of the horses).

An Amish bride's dress is typically blue or purple and is made in the same style as the dresses Amish women wear to church. The bride and her attendants wear white capes and aprons over their dresses, as well as small white *kapps* (head coverings). Amish grooms wear black suits and white shirts. Some also wear black bow ties, which are seldom worn for regular church services.

Amish weddings are usually held in the bride's home, and the service, which is similar to a regular preaching service, begins early in the morning. There is no wedding music, ring exchange, or kiss, as in traditional "English" (non-Amish) weddings. The bride and groom receive a time of counseling while their guests sing a song. During the wedding service, scriptures are read, sermons are given, and prayers are said. The bride and groom then stand before the bishop, who asks them questions, similar to what the English do during their wedding vows. At the end of the service, the wedding meal is served to all of the guests in attendance.

# Desserts

*And they gave him a piece of a cake of figs,
and two clusters of raisins: and when he had eaten,
his spirit came again to him.*

1 Samuel 30:12

Moist and Tender Chocolate Cake

2 cups flour

⅔ cup cocoa

1 teaspoon baking powder

1 teaspoon baking soda

½ teaspoon salt

¾ cup butter or margarine

1¾ cups sugar

2 teaspoons vanilla

2 large eggs

1 cup water

Preheat oven to 350°. Grease and flour two 9-inch round baking pans or one 9x13-inch baking pan. In medium bowl, combine flour, cocoa, baking powder, baking soda, and salt. In large bowl, cream butter, sugar, and vanilla. Add eggs one at a time, beating well after each addition. Gradually add flour mixture alternately with water. Spread into prepared pans. Bake for 25 to 35 minutes or until toothpick inserted in center comes out clean. Cool in pans for 15 minutes; invert onto wire racks to cool completely. Fill and frost with Chocolate Lover's Frosting (see page 48).

Chocolate Lover's Frosting

3 cups sifted powdered sugar, divided
⅔ cup cocoa
½ cup butter or margarine, softened
5 to 6 tablespoons milk, divided
1 teaspoon vanilla

In small mixing bowl, beat 1 cup powdered sugar, cocoa, butter, 2 tablespoons milk, and vanilla until creamy. Gradually beat in remaining powdered sugar and milk until smooth. Yields 2 cups.

Susanna Schrock
Wheatland, MO

Cake That Doesn't Last

3 cups flour
2 cups sugar
1 teaspoon baking soda
1 teaspoon salt
3 eggs
1½ cups vegetable oil
1 (8 ounce) can crushed pineapple, drained
1 cup nuts, chopped
1 teaspoon vanilla
2 cups mashed bananas

Preheat oven to 350°. Mix dry ingredients in large bowl. Make well in center and fill with eggs, oil, pineapple, nuts, vanilla, and bananas. Stir lightly; do not beat. Pour into greased and floured tube pan or loaf pan. Bake for 75 minutes.

Katie Miller
Pierpont, OH

*Smiles go a long way,
even at home.*

Apple Dapple Cake

2 eggs
2 cups sugar
1 cup vegetable oil
2¾ cups flour
1 teaspoon baking soda
½ teaspoon salt
3 cups chopped apples
1 teaspoon vanilla
1 cup chopped nuts (optional)

Preheat oven to 350°. Combine eggs, sugar, and oil. Sift dry ingredients
and add to egg mixture. Stir in apples, vanilla, and nuts (if desired).
Pour into greased 9x13-inch pan and bake for 30 minutes. Drizzle with
hot icing while cake is still hot.

Icing

1 cup brown sugar
2 tablespoons butter
¼ cup milk

Combine icing ingredients in saucepan and boil for 2½ minutes on
medium heat. Stir lightly after removing from heat.

Mrs. Jeremia Schwartz
Monroe, IN

Shoofly Cake

1 cup light (mild) molasses
2¼ cups boiling water
1 tablespoon baking soda
¾ cup vegetable oil
4 cups flour
1 pound light brown sugar

Preheat oven to 350°. Combine molasses, boiling water, and baking soda. In separate bowl, mix oil, flour, and sugar until mixture resembles crumbs. Reserve 1 cup crumbs for topping. Stir remaining crumbs into molasses mixture and pour into greased 9x13-inch pan. Top with reserved crumbs. Bake for 40 to 45 minutes.

Marie Martin
Ephrata, PA

• • •

Criticism is the disapproval of people, not for having faults, but for having faults different from our own.

• • •

Rhubarb Upside-Down Cake

CRUST

¼ cup butter

¾ cup packed brown sugar

3 cups diced rhubarb

2 tablespoons sugar

In small bowl, combine butter and brown sugar. Spread into greased 9-inch round baking pan. Layer with rhubarb; sprinkle with 2 tablespoons sugar.

BATTER

½ cup soft butter

1 cup sugar

2 eggs, separated

1 teaspoon vanilla

1½ cups flour

2 teaspoons baking powder

½ teaspoon salt

½ cup milk

¼ teaspoon cream of tartar

Preheat oven to 325°. Cream butter and sugar. Beat in egg yolks and vanilla. Combine flour, baking powder, and salt; add to creamed mixture alternately with milk. In small bowl, beat egg whites with cream of tartar until stiff peaks form; fold into batter. Spoon batter over rhubarb. Bake for 40 to 45 minutes or until done. Serve with whipped cream.

Gwyn Auker
Elk Horn, KY

Lemon Pudding Cake

8 eggs, separated
⅔ cup lemon juice
2 teaspoons lemon zest
2 tablespoons butter, melted
3 cups sugar
1 cup flour
1 teaspoon salt
3 cups milk

Preheat oven to 350°. Beat egg yolks, lemon juice, lemon zest, and butter. Combine sugar, flour, and salt; add to egg mixture alternately with milk. Beat egg whites until stiff and fold into batter. Pour into greased 9x13-inch pan. Set pan inside a larger pan of hot water in the oven. Bake for 45 minutes.

Ellen Yoder
Scottville, MI

> *She who receives a good turn should never forget it; she who does a good turn should never remember it.*

Fudge Pudding Cake

1 cup flour

¾ cup sugar

2 tablespoons cocoa

2 teaspoons baking powder

½ teaspoon salt

½ cup milk

2 tablespoons vegetable oil

1 teaspoon vanilla

1 cup brown sugar

¼ cup cocoa

1¾ cups hot tap water

Preheat oven to 350°. Mix flour, sugar, cocoa, baking powder, and salt in greased 9-inch square pan. Stir in milk, oil, and vanilla until smooth. Sprinkle with brown sugar and ¼ cup cocoa. Pour hot water over batter. Bake for 40 minutes. Serve warm with vanilla ice cream if desired.

Rachel Ann Stoltzfus
Gap, PA

Bernie's Birthday Cake

½ cup cocoa

1½ teaspoons baking soda

½ cup cold water

⅔ cup shortening

1¾ cups sugar

1 teaspoon vanilla

2 eggs

2½ cups sifted flour

½ teaspoon salt

¾ cup sour milk

Preheat oven to 350°. In mixing bowl, combine cocoa, baking soda, and water; let stand. In separate bowl, cream shortening and sugar. Add vanilla and eggs and beat well. Sift flour with salt then stir alternately with milk into creamed mixture. Add cocoa mixture. Pour into greased 9x13-inch pan. Bake for 35 minutes.

Ruth Martin
Selinsgrove, PA

Banana Cake

½ cup shortening

1½ cups sugar

2 eggs

I cup mashed bananas (about 3)

I teaspoon vanilla

2 cups flour

I teaspoon baking soda

⅓ teaspoon salt

½ cup sour milk or buttermilk

½ cup chopped walnuts

Preheat oven to 350°. Cream shortening and sugar. Add eggs one at a time, beating well after each addition. Mix in mashed bananas and vanilla. Sift dry ingredients together and add alternately with milk. Fold in nuts. Pour into greased 9x13-inch pan and bake for 45 minutes.

Mrs. Norman Miller
Clark, MO

Don't eat yourself too full already—there's cake back yet!

Zucchini Carrot Cake

2 cups flour
2 cups sugar
2 teaspoons cinnamon
½ teaspoon salt
I teaspoon baking powder
2 teaspoons baking soda
¾ cup vegetable oil
4 eggs
I teaspoon vanilla
2 cups shredded zucchini
I cup shredded carrots

Preheat oven to 350°. Combine flour, sugar, cinnamon, salt, baking powder, and baking soda. Add oil, eggs, and vanilla; mix well. Fold in zucchini and carrots. Pour into greased 9x13-inch pan and bake for 45 minutes. When cool, frost with Cream Cheese Frosting.

CREAM CHEESE FROSTING
½ cup butter, softened
I (8 ounce) package cream cheese, softened
3½ cups powdered sugar
I teaspoon vanilla
I cup chopped pecans (optional)

Cream butter and cream cheese. Add powdered sugar and vanilla; beat until smooth. Fold in nuts.

Mrs. Levi Miller Sr.
Clark, MO

Coconut Carrot Cake

I cup vegetable oil

2 cups sugar

3 eggs

2 cups flour

2½ teaspoons baking soda

2 teaspoons cinnamon

I teaspoon salt

1⅓ cups flaked coconut

2 cups shredded carrots

I (8 ounce) can crushed pineapple, undrained

½ cup chopped nuts

Preheat oven to 350°. Beat oil, sugar, and eggs. Add flour, baking soda, cinnamon, and salt; beat until smooth. Add coconut, carrots, pineapple, and nuts. Pour into greased 9x13-inch pan and bake for 50 to 60 minutes. When cool, frost with Coconut Frosting.

Coconut Frosting

I cup flaked coconut, divided

¼ cup margarine, softened

3 ounces cream cheese, softened

3 cups powdered sugar

I tablespoon milk

½ teaspoon vanilla

Toast coconut; cool. Cream margarine and cream cheese. Add powdered sugar alternately with milk and vanilla; beat until smooth. Add half the toasted coconut. Frost cake. Top with remaining coconut.

Laura Byler
Woodhull, NY

German Raw Apple Cake

½ cup butter or margarine

½ cup brown sugar

1 cup sugar

2¼ cups flour

¼ teaspoon salt

1 teaspoon cinnamon

2 teaspoons baking soda

1 cup sour milk (1 tablespoon vinegar plus enough milk to make 1 cup)

2 cups diced raw apples

TOPPING

½ cup sugar

½ teaspoon cinnamon

¼ cup brown sugar

Chopped nuts (optional)

Preheat oven to 350°. Cream butter and sugars. Combine flour, salt, and cinnamon. Add baking soda to sour milk. Add dry ingredients and sour milk to creamed mixture and stir well. Fold in apples. Pour into greased 9x13-inch pan. Combine topping ingredients and sprinkle evenly on top. Bake for 40 minutes.

Jeannie Martin
Newville, PA

Maple Nut Angel Food Cake

2 cups egg whites
¼ cup water
¾ teaspoon salt
2 teaspoons cream of tartar
2¼ cups brown sugar, divided
1½ cups flour
2 tablespoons cornstarch
½ teaspoon maple extract
1 teaspoon vanilla
½ cup chopped nuts

Preheat oven to 375°. In mixing bowl, beat egg whites, water, salt, and cream of tartar until smooth. Add half the brown sugar and beat until stiff. Combine flour, remaining brown sugar, and cornstarch; fold into stiff batter. Add maple extract, vanilla, and nuts. (May substitute 1¾ cups cake flour for the all-purpose flour; omit cornstarch if doing so.) Pour into angel food cake pan and bake for 35 to 40 minutes.

Sarah Miller
Fredonia, PA

Coconut Blueberry Cake

2 cups flour
1 cup sugar
3 teaspoons baking powder
¼ teaspoon salt
2 eggs
1 cup milk
½ cup vegetable oil
1½ cups fresh or frozen blueberries
1 cup flaked coconut

Preheat oven to 375°. In mixing bowl, combine flour, sugar, baking powder, and salt. In separate bowl, beat eggs, milk, and oil; stir into dry ingredients just until moistened. Fold in blueberries. Pour into greased 9x13-inch pan. Sprinkle with coconut. Bake for 22 to 24 minutes or until toothpick inserted in center comes out clean.

Regina Gingerich
LaValle, WI

● ● ●

No one has ever choked to death by swallowing her pride.

● ● ●

Sour Cream Spice Cake

½ cup shortening	2 teaspoons cinnamon
2 cups brown sugar	I teaspoon cloves
3 eggs, separated	I teaspoon allspice
I cup sour cream	½ teaspoon salt
1¾ cups flour	I teaspoon vanilla

Preheat oven to 350°. Cream shortening and sugar. Add egg yolks and sour cream; mix well. Combine flour, baking soda, cinnamon, cloves, allspice, and salt; add to creamed mixture and beat well. Add vanilla. Beat egg whites until stiff and fold into batter. Pour into greased 13x9-inch pan and bake for 25 minutes. When cool, frost with Caramel Icing.

CARAMEL ICING

I cup brown sugar

2 tablespoons butter

Pinch of salt

3 tablespoons shortening

¼ cup milk

1½ cups powdered sugar

I teaspoon vanilla

In saucepan, bring sugar, butter, salt, and shortening to a boil; add milk. Boil slowly for 3 minutes. Remove from heat and cool. Add powdered sugar and beat well. Stir in vanilla.

Bad habits are like a comfortable bed: easy to get into and hard to get out of.

Mary Ann Yoder
Woodhull, NY

Pumpkin Sheet Cake

1 (16 ounce) can pumpkin

2 cups sugar

1 cup vegetable oil

4 eggs, lightly beaten

2 cups flour

2 teaspoons baking soda

1 teaspoon cinnamon

½ teaspoon salt

Preheat oven to 350°. In mixing bowl, beat pumpkin, sugar, and oil. Add eggs and mix well. Combine flour, baking soda, cinnamon, and salt. Add to pumpkin mixture and beat until well blended. Pour into greased 10x15-inch baking pan. Bake for 25 to 30 minutes or until cake tests done. When cool, frost with Cream Cheese Frosting.

CREAM CHEESE FROSTING

5 tablespoons butter or margarine, softened

3 ounces cream cheese, softened

1 teaspoon vanilla

1¾ cups powdered sugar

3 to 4 teaspoons milk

Chopped nuts

Beat butter, cream cheese, and vanilla in mixing bowl until smooth. Gradually add powdered sugar. Mix well. Add milk until frosting reaches desired spreading consistency. Frost cake and sprinkle with nuts.

Clara Miller
Fredericktown, OH

Oatmeal Cake

½ cup butter

1 cup boiling water

1 cup sugar

1 cup brown sugar

1½ cups flour

1 cup rolled oats

1 teaspoon baking soda

Pinch of salt

2 eggs

1 teaspoon vanilla

Preheat oven to 350°. Mix together butter, boiling water, and sugars; let set until butter melts. Combine flour, oats, baking soda, and salt; add to sugar mixture. Add eggs and vanilla; mix well. Pour into greased 8x12-inch pan and bake for 30 to 35 minutes.

Mrs. Dan Swartzentruber
Newcomerstown, OH

Applesauce Cake

½ cup shortening

2 cups sugar

½ cup water

2 eggs, beaten

1½ cups applesauce

2 cups flour

1½ teaspoons baking powder

1½ teaspoons baking soda

1 teaspoon salt

¾ teaspoon cinnamon

½ teaspoon cloves

½ teaspoon allspice

1 cup raisins

½ cup chopped nuts

Preheat oven to 350°. Cream shortening and sugar. Add water, eggs, and applesauce to creamed mixture. Combine flour, baking powder, baking soda, salt, cinnamon, cloves, and allspice; add to batter and mix well. Stir in raisins and nuts. Pour into greased 9-inch square pan and bake for 35 to 40 minutes.

Mary Raber
Holmesville, OH

Rhubarb Coffee Cake

½ cup shortening

1½ cups brown sugar

1 egg

1 cup sour cream

2½ cups flour

1 teaspoon baking soda

Pinch of salt

2 cups chopped rhubarb

Topping

¼ cup sugar

¼ cup brown sugar

½ cup nuts, chopped

1 teaspoon cinnamon

1 tablespoon butter

Preheat oven to 350°. Cream shortening and sugar; add egg and beat well. Add sour cream, flour, baking soda, salt, and rhubarb. Pour into greased 9x13-inch pan. Combine topping ingredients and sprinkle evenly on top. Bake for 45 minutes or until cake tests done.

Ida Miller
Smicksburg, PA

Wanda's Caramel Candy

¾ cup light corn syrup
2 cups brown sugar
½ cup butter
2 cups whipping cream, divided

Combine all ingredients except 1 cup whipping cream in saucepan and bring to a boil; gradually add remaining cream. Bring to a hard boil and cook until mixture reaches hard-ball stage. Pour into buttered 9x13-inch pan. Let cool. Cut into squares.

Mandy Schwartz
Portland, IN

Mocha Truffles

2 (12 ounce) packages semisweet chocolate chips
1 (8 ounce) package cream cheese
3 tablespoons instant coffee granules
2 teaspoons water
Additional semisweet chocolate chips, melted

In saucepan, melt chocolate chips. Add cream cheese, coffee, and water; mix well. Chill until firm enough to shape. Shape into 1-inch balls and place on cookie sheet lined with wax paper. Chill for 1 to 2 hours or until firm. Dip in additional melted chocolate. Yields about 5½ dozen truffles.

Sarah Troyer
Mercer, PA

Marbled Orange Fudge

¾ cup butter (no substitutes)
3 cups sugar
¾ cup whipping cream
1 package vanilla or white chips
1 (7 ounce) jar marshmallow crème
3 teaspoons orange extract
12 drops yellow food coloring
5 drops red food coloring

In heavy saucepan, combine butter, sugar, and whipping cream. Cook and stir on low heat until sugar is dissolved. Bring to a boil; cook and stir for 4 minutes. Remove from heat; stir in chips and marshmallow crème. Remove 1 cup and set aside. Add orange extract and colorings to remaining mixture. Stir until blended. Pour into greased 13x9-inch pan. Drop reserved mixture by tablespoons on top and cut through with a knife to swirl.

Linda Peachey
Beaver, OH

Goat's Milk Fudge

3 cups sugar
1 cup goat's milk
¼ cup light corn syrup
1 tablespoon butter
1 pound chocolate or white almond bark coating
1 teaspoon vanilla or maple extract
Chopped nuts (optional)

In saucepan, combine sugar, milk, and light corn syrup; bring to a boil.
Cook until almost to soft-ball stage. Remove pan from heat and set in
bowl of cold water until mixture becomes thick around the edges. Add
1 tablespoon butter and 1 pound almond bark coating; stir until glossy.
Add vanilla or maple extract. Add nuts if desired.

Mrs. David Sommers
La Plata, MO

*It isn't your
position that makes you
happy; it's your disposition.*

Peanut Butter Fudge

I cup margarine
I cup crunchy peanut butter
4 cups powdered sugar
I teaspoon vanilla

In saucepan, melt margarine and add peanut butter, powdered sugar, and vanilla. Beat well until smooth. Pour into greased 8-inch square pan. Refrigerate for 3 hours.

Marie Troyer
Mercer, PA

Frozen Fudge

1½ cups milk
½ cup cream
½ cup sugar
3 tablespoons cocoa
½ teaspoon vanilla
Pinch of salt

Combine all ingredients and blend until smooth. Pour into ice cube tray and freeze overnight or until hard. Thaw for 5 to 10 minutes before serving.

Clara Yoder
Windsor, MO

Peppermint Patties

½ cup warm mashed potatoes (mashed with
    milk only)
1 tablespoon shortening
3½ cups powdered sugar
7 drops peppermint extract
Dark sweet chocolate, melted

Beat all ingredients until smooth. Add additional powdered sugar if needed to reach desired consistency. Shape into patties and freeze. Coat patties with melted chocolate while frozen. Note: This recipe won a first-place ribbon at the Malheur County Fair in Ontario, Oregon. It also won the grand prize in the candy division.

Bertha Stauffer
Mechanicsville, MO

Yum Yums

¼ cup butter, softened
2 cups peanut butter
2 cups powdered sugar
3 cups crispy rice cereal
Semisweet chocolate chips, melted

Combine butter, peanut butter, and powdered sugar; add crispy rice cereal and stir until combined. Roll into balls. Dip in melted chocolate.

Katie Zook
Apple Creek, OH

♦ ♦ ♦

No person can do everything, but each one can do something.

♦ ♦ ♦

Coconut Bonbons

2 cups sugar
2 cups light corn syrup
¼ cup butter or margarine
2 cups flaked coconut
Semisweet chocolate chips, melted

Combine sugar, light corn syrup, and butter in saucepan. Bring to a boil until mixture reaches hard-ball stage. Remove from heat and stir in coconut. Cool and shape into balls. Dip in melted chocolate.

Barbara Miller
Port Washington, OH

Strawberry Divinity

3 cups sugar
¾ cup light corn syrup
¾ cup water
2 egg whites
1 (3 ounce) package strawberry gelatin
1 cup chopped nuts

Combine sugar, light corn syrup, and water in heavy 3-quart saucepan. Cook on medium heat, stirring constantly, until sugar is dissolved. If sugar crystals form on sides of pan, wipe them off. Continue cooking until mixture reaches hard-ball stage (252°). Meanwhile, beat egg whites until stiff but not dry. Blend gelatin into egg whites. When syrup reaches 252°, pour slowly over egg white mixture, beating constantly on medium speed. Beat as long as possible, using wooden spoon if mixture becomes too stiff for mixer. Add nuts and spread into lightly buttered 9-inch square pan. When cool and firm, cut into 36 pieces. Yields about 2 pounds.

Cora Hershberger
Burton, OH

Buttermilk Cookies

2 cups butter or margarine

3 cups brown sugar

1 cup sugar

3 eggs

4 teaspoons baking powder

4 teaspoons baking soda

4 teaspoons vanilla

1½ cups buttermilk or sour milk

8 cups flour

Preheat oven to 350°. Cream butter and sugars. Add eggs, baking powder, baking soda, and vanilla; mix well. Add buttermilk (or sour milk) alternately with flour until well blended. Drop by teaspoons onto well-greased cookie sheet and bake for 11 to 13 minutes. Let set for 5 minutes before removing from cookie sheet. Note: To sour milk, add 1 teaspoon vinegar to each cup of milk. This recipe won a first-place ribbon at the Malheur County Fair in Ontario, Oregon.

Emma Raber
Holmesville, OH

Maple Syrup Cookies

1 teaspoon baking soda
1 tablespoon milk
1 egg
½ cup plus 2 tablespoons shortening
1 cup maple syrup
3 cups flour
3 teaspoons baking powder
½ teaspoon salt
1 teaspoon vanilla
1 (8 ounce) package semisweet chocolate chips

Preheat oven to 350°. In small cup, dissolve baking soda in milk and set aside. Cream egg, shortening, and syrup. Add flour, baking powder, salt, vanilla, and baking soda mixture; blend well. Stir in chocolate chips. Drop by teaspoons onto greased cookie sheet and bake for 12 to 15 minutes.

Mattie Ann Miller
Medford, WI

Frosted Rhubarb Cookies

1 cup shortening
1½ cups packed brown sugar
2 eggs
3 cups flour
1 teaspoon baking soda
½ teaspoon salt
1½ cups diced rhubarb
¾ cup flaked coconut

Preheat oven to 350°. In large bowl, cream shortening and brown sugar. Beat in eggs. Combine flour, baking soda, and salt; add to creamed mixture. Fold in rhubarb and coconut. Drop by rounded tablespoons 2 inches apart onto greased cookie sheet. Bake for 10 to 14 minutes or until golden brown. When cool, spread with Cream Cheese Frosting.

CREAM CHEESE FROSTING
3 ounces cream cheese
1 tablespoon butter, softened
1 ½ cups powdered sugar
3 teaspoons vanilla

Combine frosting ingredients and blend until smooth.

Gwyn Auker
Elk Horn, KY

Never-Fail Cookies

1½ cups shortening
1 cup sugar
1 cup brown sugar
2 eggs
2 teaspoons baking powder
2 teaspoons baking soda
2 tablespoons vinegar
2 teaspoons vanilla
1 teaspoon almond extract
4 cups flour

Preheat oven to 350°. Cream shortening and sugars. Add eggs and beat well. Dissolve baking powder and baking soda in vinegar and add to creamed mixture along with vanilla and almond extract; mix well. Add flour last and beat until well blended. Shape into balls and place on greased cookie sheet. Press down with tines of fork. Bake for 15 to 20 minutes. Do not overbake.

Anna Stutzman
Arcola, IL

No-Bake Oatmeal Turtle Cookies

½ cup margarine
1½ cups sugar
½ cup evaporated milk
5 tablespoons cocoa
½ cup peanut butter
1 teaspoon vanilla
3 cups rolled oats

In medium heavy saucepan, bring margarine, sugar, milk, and cocoa to a boil. Boil for 1 minute, stirring constantly. Be careful not to burn mixture. Remove from heat and stir in peanut butter, vanilla, and oats. Mix quickly and drop by teaspoons onto cookie sheet lined with waxed paper. Let cool. Yields about 3 dozen cookies.

Mary Miller
Heuvelton, NY

• • •

No one has the right to do as she pleases unless she pleases to do what is right.

• • •

Diabetic Sugar-Free Raisin Bars

I cup raisins

½ cup water

½ cup margarine

I teaspoon cinnamon

¼ teaspoon nutmeg

I egg, slightly beaten

¾ cup unsweetened applesauce

¼ teaspoon vanilla

I cup flour

I tablespoon sugar substitute

I teaspoon baking soda

Preheat oven to 350°. In saucepan on medium heat, cook raisins, water, margarine, cinnamon, and nutmeg until margarine is melted. Continue cooking for 3 minutes. Add egg, applesauce, and vanilla and mix well. Combine flour, sugar substitute, and baking soda to cooked mixture and stir. Spread into greased 8-inch square pan and bake for 25 to 30 minutes or until lightly browned. Cut into bars.

Ellen Schwartz
Stanwood, MI

Vanishing Oatmeal Raisin Cookies

1 cup butter or margarine, softened

1 cup packed brown sugar

½ cup sugar

2 eggs

1 teaspoon vanilla

1½ cups flour

1 teaspoon baking soda

1 teaspoon cinnamon

½ teaspoon salt

3 cups quick oats

1 cup raisins

Preheat oven to 350°. Cream butter and sugars. Add eggs and vanilla and beat well. Combine flour, baking soda, cinnamon, and salt; mix well. Stir in oats and raisins. Drop by rounded tablespoons onto greased cookie sheet. Bake for 10 to 12 minutes or until golden brown. Cool for 1 minute on cookie sheet before removing to wire rack. Yields about 4 dozen cookies. Variation: To make bar cookies, spread batter into ungreased 9x13-inch baking pan and bake for 30 to 35 minutes. Cut into bars.

Mrs. Ervin Miller
Clark, MO

Chewy Chocolate Chip Bars

I cup butter or margarine,
  softened
I cup brown sugar, divided
½ cup white sugar
I tablespoon water
I teaspoon vanilla
2 eggs, separated

2 cups flour
I teaspoon baking powder
½ teaspoon baking soda
½ teaspoon salt
¾ cup semisweet chocolate chips
¾ cup finely chopped walnuts

Preheat oven to 350°. In mixing bowl, cream butter, ½ cup brown sugar, and white sugar until light and fluffy. Add water, vanilla, and egg yolks (reserve whites in separate bowl). Beat for 2 to 3 minutes. Beat in flour, baking powder, baking soda, and salt. Spread into lightly greased 9x13-inch baking pan. Sprinkle with chocolate chips. Beat egg whites until soft peaks form; add remaining ½ cup brown sugar and blend well. Carefully spread over chocolate chips. Sprinkle with chopped nuts. Bake for 35 minutes or until meringue is golden brown. Cut with a sharp knife while still hot. Yields 3 dozen bars.

Anna Yoder
Laurenceburg, TN

Oatmeal Whoopie Pies

¾ cup butter

2 cups brown sugar

2 eggs

2 cups flour

½ teaspoon salt

I teaspoon baking powder

2 cups quick cooking oats

I teaspoon cinnamon

2 teaspoons baking soda

3 tablespoons boiling water

Preheat oven to 325°. Cream butter, sugar, and eggs. Combine flour, salt, and baking powder and add to creamed mixture. Add oats and cinnamon; mix well. Stir baking soda into boiling water; add to batter and blend well. Drop by tablespoons onto greased cookie sheet and bake for 10 to 15 minutes. Cool and fill.

FILLING

5 tablespoons flour

I cup milk

I cup powdered sugar

½ teaspoon vanilla

¼ cup margarine

¼ cup shortening

Cook flour and milk until mixture forms a smooth paste. Cool. Add remaining ingredients and beat until mixture resembles whipped cream. Spread between two cookies. Note: Cookies are best frozen and eaten directly from the freezer.

Lena Bender
McVeytown, PA

Grassroot Dream Cookies

½ cup margarine
½ cup sugar
½ cup packed brown sugar
I egg
¾ teaspoon vanilla
I cup flour
I teaspoon baking powder
¼ teaspoon baking soda
¼ teaspoon salt
½ cup rolled oats
I cup cornflakes
½ cup flaked coconut

Preheat oven to 325°. Cream margarine and sugars. Add egg and vanilla; blend until smooth. Sift flour, baking powder, baking soda, and salt; add to creamed mixture. Stir in rolled oats, cornflakes, and coconut. Drop by teaspoons onto lightly greased cookie sheet. Bake for 12 to 15 minutes. Yields 5 dozen crisp 2-inch cookies.

Susanna Schrock
Wheatland, MO

Raisin Molasses Cookies

2 cups raisins
1 cup shortening
½ cup sugar
2 eggs
1½ cups molasses
4 cups flour
3 teaspoons baking powder
½ teaspoon baking soda
1 teaspoon salt
2 teaspoons cinnamon
2 teaspoons ginger

Rinse and drain raisins. Cream shortening and sugar. Add eggs and beat well. Blend in molasses. Sift flour with baking powder, baking soda, salt, cinnamon, and ginger. Blend into creamed mixture. Stir in raisins. Drop by teaspoons onto greased cookie sheet and bake for 15 to 18 minutes. Yields about 6 dozen cookies.

Martha Byler
Spartansburg, PA

Hand-Cranked French Strawberry Ice Cream

6 egg yolks
2 cups milk
1 cup sugar
Pinch of salt
4 cups heavy cream
2 cups crushed strawberries
1 tablespoon lemon juice

Mix egg yolks, milk, sugar, and salt in double boiler and heat until mixture forms a thick custard. Cook until mixture coats the back of a wooden spoon evenly. Allow to cool. Add heavy cream. Pour into ice cream freezer and crank until half frozen. Add crushed strawberries and lemon juice and continue to crank until frozen. Allow to ripen (sit) a few hours before serving. Yields 2½ quarts.

Mollie Stoltzfus
Charlotte Hall, MD

♦ ♦ ♦

Don't ask God for what yo
think is good;
ask Him for what He thinl
is good for you.

♦ ♦ ♦

School Ice Cream

9 eggs

3 tablespoons gelatin

3¾ cups milk, divided

2 (3 ounce) packages instant pudding mix (any flavor)

2 quarts cream or milk

2½ cups sugar

½ cup brown sugar

2 tablespoons vanilla

In mixing bowl, beat eggs well. Soak gelatin in ¾ cup cold milk. Heat remaining 3 cups milk; add gelatin mixture and stir until dissolved. Add pudding mix, cream, sugars, and vanilla to egg mixture; beat well. Pour into ice cream freezer and process until frozen.

Lena Byler
Atlantic, PA

Vanilla Ice Cream

1 quart cream
8 eggs
2 (3 ounce) packages vanilla instant pudding mix
2 cans evaporated milk
½ cup brown sugar
1½ cups sugar

Whip cream. In separate bowl, beat eggs well; add to whipped cream. Mix pudding according to package directions and add to whipped cream and eggs. Add evaporated milk and pour into 2-gallon ice cream freezer. Fill up with milk. Process until ice cream is frozen.

Sarah Miller
Dundee, OH

Sherbet

2 cups hot water
2 (6 ounce) packages gelatin (any flavor)
½ cup sugar
2 quarts milk

Dissolve gelatin in water and chill until partially set. Add sugar and milk; beat well. Pour into ice cream freezer and process until frozen.

Lovina Hershberger
Dalton, OH

Chocolate Sauce

I cup sugar
2 tablespoons butter or margarine
¼ cup cream or milk
4 tablespoons light corn syrup or maple syrup
2 scant tablespoons cocoa

Combine all ingredients in saucepan and bring to a boil. Cook for 3 minutes and serve over ice cream.

Mattie Ann Miller
Medford, WI

A smile is a very powerful weapon; you can even break ice with it.

Butterscotch Topping

3 teaspoons butter

1 cup sugar

1 cup brown sugar

½ teaspoon salt

½ cup milk

1 teaspoon vanilla

Melt butter in saucepan and add sugars, salt, and milk. Cook for 2 minutes. Add vanilla.

Lydia Troyer
Mercer, PA

A smile adds a
great deal to
face value.

Funny Cake Pie

CAKE BATTER

1¼ cups flour

¾ cup sugar

2 teaspoons baking powder

¼ cup shortening

I egg

½ cup milk

½ teaspoon vanilla

Preheat oven to 350°. Combine cake batter ingredients and set aside.

BASE

I cup sugar

¼ cup cocoa

¾ cup hot water

I teaspoon vanilla

I (9 inch) unbaked pie shell

Combine sugar, cocoa, water, and vanilla and pour into unbaked pie shell. Carefully pour cake batter on top. Bake for 45 minutes.

Miriam Brunstetter
Easton, PA

Coconut Oatmeal Pie

1 cup light corn syrup
½ cup brown sugar
⅓ cup butter, melted
1 teaspoon vanilla
⅓ teaspoon salt
3 eggs, beaten
½ cup flaked coconut
½ cup oatmeal
1 (9 inch) unbaked pie shell

Preheat oven to 350°. Combine all ingredients in order given and mix well. Pour into unbaked pie shell and bake for 30 to 35 minutes or until pie tests done.

Mrs. John Miller
Navarre, OH

Learn to be smart in the things that matter; give blessings to others, and let your love scatter.

Shoofly Pie

2 cups cane molasses
2 cups warm water
I tablespoon baking soda
4 (9 inch) unbaked pie shells

Preheat oven to 350°. Combine molasses, water, and baking soda. Divide mixture equally into unbaked pie shells. Divide crumbs and sprinkle evenly on top of filling in pie shells; let stand for 10 minutes. Bake for 30 to 40 minutes or until done.

CRUMB MIXTURE

4 cups flour
2 cups sugar
3 tablespoons butter
3 tablespoons lard or shortening
I teaspoon cinnamon
¾ teaspoon nutmeg
¾ teaspoon ginger
Pinch of salt

Blend all ingredients until mixture forms crumbs. Note: Butter and lard (or shortening) tablespoon measurements should be level. Crumbs will be dry.

Mattie Hershberger
Heuvelton, NY

Lemon Shoofly Pie

1 egg
Zest of 2 lemons
Juice of 2 lemons, strained
2 tablespoons flour
½ cup sugar
½ cup molasses
¾ cup boiling water
1 (9 inch) unbaked pie shell

Preheat oven to 350°. Combine all ingredients and pour into unbaked pie shell. Sprinkle crumbs evenly on top of filling. Bake for 45 to 60 minutes. Note: This recipe won a first-place ribbon at the Malheur County Fair in Ontario, Oregon.

CRUMB MIXTURE
1½ cups flour
½ cup sugar
½ cup shortening
    or butter, softened
½ teaspoon baking
    soda

Blend all ingredients until mixture forms crumbs.

Mom's shoofly pie is wonderful good!

Mrs. Henry Leid
Elkton, KY

Chocolate Shoofly Pie

1 quart milk or water
1¼ cups sugar
2 tablespoons cocoa
5 tablespoons cornstarch
1 tablespoon butter
1 teaspoon vanilla
4 (8 inch) unbaked pie shells

Preheat oven to 325°. In saucepan, combine milk, sugar, cocoa, and cornstarch; cook until thickened. Add butter and vanilla; cool. Divide mixture equally into unbaked pie shells. Pour topping over filling and bake for 1 hour.

TOPPING
2 cups flour
2 cups sugar
¾ cup cocoa
2 teaspoons baking powder
2 teaspoons baking soda
1 cup milk
1 cup hot coffee
½ cup vegetable oil
2 eggs
1 teaspoon vanilla
Dash of salt

Combine topping ingredients and beat well.

Linda Esh
Paradise, PA

95

Vanilla Crumb Pie

1 cup brown sugar

1 cup light corn syrup

2 cups water

2 tablespoons flour

1 egg

½ teaspoon cream of tartar

1 teaspoon vanilla

1 teaspoon baking soda

3 (9 inch) unbaked pie shells

Preheat oven to 375°. In saucepan, combine brown sugar, light corn syrup, water, and flour. Bring to a boil for 1 minute; set aside. In large bowl, beat egg, cream of tartar, vanilla, and baking soda; add to cooked mixture. Divide mixture equally into unbaked pie shells.

CRUMB MIXTURE

2 cups flour

1 cup brown sugar

½ cup lard

1 teaspoon cream of tartar

½ teaspoon baking powder

Blend all ingredients until mixture forms crumbs. Divide crumbs and sprinkle evenly on top of filling in pie shells. Bake for 45 minutes.

Mahala Miller
Medford, WI

No-Crust Apple Pie

1 egg
½ cup flour
1 teaspoon baking powder
Dash of salt
2 medium apples, sliced
½ cup brown sugar
1 teaspoon vanilla
½ cup chopped nuts (optional)

Preheat oven to 350°. In mixing bowl, beat egg and add remaining ingredients; mix well. Spread into greased pie pan and bake for 30 minutes or until apples are soft.

Clara Yoder
Windsor, MO

*The extra mile
is never crowded.*

Pilgrim Pie

¼ cup margarine

1 cup sugar

2 eggs

1 cup light corn syrup

½ cup water

1 teaspoon vanilla

1 cup flaked coconut

1 cup rolled oats

½ teaspoon salt

1 (9 inch) unbaked pie shell

Preheat oven to 450°. Cream margarine and sugar. Add remaining ingredients and mix well. Pour into unbaked pie shell and bake at 450° for 10 minutes and then at 350° for 30 minutes.

Mrs. Chris Beachy
McIntire, IA

● ● ●

There is no teaching to compare with example.

● ● ●

Rhubarb Cream Pie

2 tablespoons butter
2 cups chopped rhubarb
½ cup water
1¼ cups sugar, divided
2 heaping tablespoons cornstarch
⅛ teaspoon salt
2 eggs, separated
¼ cup cream or rich milk
6 tablespoons sugar
1 teaspoon lemon juice
1 (9 inch) baked pie shell

Preheat oven to 400°. In large saucepan, melt butter; add rhubarb, water, and 1 cup sugar. Cook slowly until rhubarb is tender. In mixing bowl, combine ¼ cup sugar, cornstarch, salt, egg yolks, and cream. Add to rhubarb mixture and cook until thick. Pour into baked pie crust. To make meringue, beat egg whites until stiff. Add 6 tablespoons sugar and 1 teaspoon lemon juice. Pile on top of pie. Bake for 8 to 10 minutes or until browned.

Mrs. Miller
Morley, MI

Raisin Cream Pie

3 cups milk
1 cup sugar
3 heaping tablespoons flour
¾ teaspoon salt
6 egg yolks
¼ cup butter or margarine
1 cup cooked raisins
3 teaspoons vanilla
2 (9 inch) baked pie shells
1 (12 ounce) carton frozen whipped topping, thawed

Heat milk in saucepan. Combine sugar, flour, and salt. Add egg yolks and enough milk to form a smooth paste. Add paste mixture to heated milk and stir constantly until thick. Remove from heat and add butter, cooked raisins, and vanilla. Cool. Pour into baked pie shells. Top with whipped topping.

Anna Beechy
Topeka, IN

Lemon Sponge Pie

9 eggs, separated
3½ cups sugar
9 tablespoons flour
Pinch of salt
Zest and juice of 3 lemons
4 tablespoons butter
6 cups milk, scalded
4 (9 inch) unbaked pie shells

Preheat oven to 425°. Combine egg yolks, sugar, flour, and salt. Mix well. Add lemon rind, lemon juice, butter, and scalded milk; mix well. Beat egg whites until stiff and fold into milk mixture. Pour into unbaked pie shells. Bake at 425° for 15 minutes; reduce heat to 325° and bake until filling is firm.

Ida Miller
Medford, WI

There's no telling how far a kind look or deed will travel.

Funeral Pie

1 cup raisins

2 cups hot water

1¼ cups sugar

4 tablespoons flour

1 egg, well beaten

Zest and juice of 1 lemon

¼ teaspoon salt

1 tablespoon butter

1 (8 inch) unbaked pie shell and pastry strips for
  lattice top

Preheat oven to 450°. Wash raisins and soak in hot water for 1 hour or longer. Drain. Add remaining ingredients and mix thoroughly. Cook in top of double boiler until thickened. Cool. Pour into pie shell and weave pastry strips over filling to make lattice top. Bake at 450° for 10 minutes; lower temperature to 350° and continue baking until pastry is nicely browned.

Esther Stauffer
Port Trevorton, PA

Key Lime Pie

CRUST

1⅓ cups graham cracker crumbs

6 tablespoons butter, melted

Preheat oven to 350°. Combine graham cracker crumbs and melted butter. Press mixture against sides and bottom of 9-inch pie pan. Bake for 5 minutes. Cool completely.

FILLING

3 egg yolks

1 (14 ounce) can sweetened condensed milk

½ cup fresh lime juice

1 teaspoon lime zest

1 cup heavy cream

Beat egg yolks until thick, about 4 minutes. Beat in condensed milk, lime juice, and lime zest. Pour into cooled graham cracker crust. Cover and refrigerate for at least 4 hours. Before serving, beat heavy cream until stiff (do not sweeten) and spoon over pie.

Mollie Stoltzfus
Charlotte Hall, MD

Experience is something you don't get until after you need it.

Magic Mocha Pudding

1½ cups flour

1 cup sugar

2 teaspoons instant coffee granules

1 egg

2½ teaspoons baking powder

½ teaspoon salt

6 tablespoons butter

1 cup milk

Vanilla to taste

Preheat oven to 350°. Combine all ingredients and mix well. Pour into baking dish. Pour half the chocolate sauce over batter and bake for 30 to 35 minutes. Add remaining sauce before serving. Serve hot with milk or cold with whipped cream.

CHOCOLATE SAUCE

1 cup sugar

2 tablespoons cocoa

1½ tablespoons cornstarch

2½ cups water

Combine sauce ingredients in saucepan and boil until thickened.

Mrs. Gid Miller
Norwalk, WI

Raspberry Tapioca Pudding

1 (10 ounce) package frozen sweetened
  raspberries, thawed
1 cup purple grape juice
⅓ cup sugar
1 (1 inch) strip lemon peel
¼ cup quick-cooking tapioca
½ cup whipping cream
2 tablespoons powdered sugar

Mash and strain raspberries, reserving juice. Discard seeds. Add enough
water to juice to measure 2 cups. Pour into large saucepan; add grape
juice, sugar, and lemon peel. Bring to a boil; reduce heat and simmer,
uncovered, for 10 minutes. Remove lemon peel. Add tapioca and cook
and stir for 10 minutes. Pour into custard cups. Cover and refrigerate
for 4 hours or until set. In mixing bowl, beat whipping
cream and powdered sugar until soft peaks
form. Serve with pudding.

Edna Nisley
Baltic, OH

> *The Lord is pleased with
> the little you have if it's
> the best you have.*

Butterscotch Tapioca Pudding

6 cups boiling water

½ teaspoon salt

1½ cups pearl tapioca

2 cups brown sugar

2 eggs, beaten

½ cup sugar

1 cup milk

½ cup margarine, browned

1 teaspoon vanilla

2 to 3 bananas, sliced

1 (8 ounce) carton frozen whipped topping, thawed

Combine water, salt, and tapioca; cook for 15 minutes. Add brown sugar and cook until tapioca is clear. In small bowl, mix together eggs, sugar, and milk; add to tapioca mixture. Cook until mixture bubbles. Add browned margarine and vanilla to pudding. Cool. Top with bananas and whipped topping.

Sarah Miller
Navarre, OH

Apple Tapioca Pudding

1 cup raisins
2 quarts water
½ cup minute tapioca
½ cup sugar
8 cups peeled and sliced apples
1 cup sugar (white or brown)
1 teaspoon cinnamon

Preheat oven to 375°. In saucepan, bring raisins and water to a boil.
Combine tapioca and sugar and add to water, stirring constantly. Boil
for 3 to 5 minutes. Remove from heat. Mix sliced apples with sugar and
cinnamon and spread in large greased baking or roasting pan. Pour tapioca mixture over apple mixture. Bake for 45 minutes or until apples are
soft.

Mrs. Noah Shirk
Liberty, KY

> ◆ ◆ ◆
>
> *The best place to find
> a helping hand is at
> the end of your arm.*
>
> ◆ ◆ ◆

Rhubarb Pudding

4 cups sliced rhubarb
1 cup water
¾ cup sugar
3 tablespoons minute tapioca
2 tablespoons margarine
2 teaspoons orange juice
⅓ teaspoon salt

Combine all ingredients in saucepan and let stand for 5 minutes. Heat to boiling and boil for 1 minute. Reduce heat and simmer for 5 minutes. Cool and serve.

Mary Miller
Heuvelton, NY

Whoever gossips to you will gossip of you.

Blackberry Pudding Cobbler

⅓ cup butter

2 cups sugar, divided

2 cups flour

1 teaspoon salt

2 teaspoons baking powder

1 cup milk

2 cups fresh or frozen blackberries

2 cups boiling water

Preheat oven to 350°. Cream butter and 1 cup sugar. Add flour, salt, baking powder, and milk to creamed mixture. Mix well and spread into a greased 9x13-inch pan. Pour blackberries on top of batter. Combine remaining 1 cup sugar and 2 cups boiling water and pour over berries. (May add more blackberries or liquid according to taste.) Bake for 50 minutes. Note: Other fruit or berries may be substituted for the black-berries.

Mrs. Paul Schrock
Marion, MI

Stove-Top Custard

2 cups milk
2 eggs, beaten
½ cup sugar (or less)
1 teaspoon vanilla
Dash of salt
Dash of nutmeg

Mix all ingredients just until blended. Pour into four custard cups (or coffee cups) and set cups in a kettle with an inch or two of cold water (pan should have a tight-fitting lid). Bring to a boil, turn off heat, and let set for 45 minutes. Unbelievable, but this makes perfect custard.

Clara Yoder
Windsor, MO

If you lose your temper, it's a sign that you have wrong on your side.

Blueberry Buckle

¾ cup sugar

¼ cup vegetable shortening

2 eggs

½ cup milk

1½ cups flour

2 teaspoons baking powder

¼ teaspoon nutmeg

Scant ¼ teaspoon cloves

½ teaspoon salt

1⅓ cups fresh blueberries

Preheat oven to 375°. Mix sugar, shortening, eggs, and milk. Stir in all dry ingredients. Fold in blueberries and spread into greased 9-inch square pan. Sprinkle batter with topping. Bake for 45 to 50 minutes. Serve warm with milk.

TOPPING

½ cup sugar

½ cup chopped nuts

⅓ cup flour

½ teaspoon cinnamon

¼ cup butter

Mix topping ingredients until crumbly and sprinkle over batter.

Mrs. Gid Miller
Norwalk, WI

Apple Walnut Cobbler

1¼ cups sugar, divided
½ teaspoon cinnamon
¾ cup coarsely chopped walnuts, divided
4 cups sliced tart apples
1 cup flour
1 teaspoon baking powder
¼ teaspoon salt
1 egg, well beaten
½ cup evaporated milk
⅓ cup margarine, melted

Preheat oven to 325°. Mix ½ cup sugar, cinnamon, and ½ cup nuts. Place apples in bottom of greased 8-inch square baking dish. Sprinkle with cinnamon mixture. Sift together remaining ¾ cup sugar, flour, baking powder, and salt. In mixing bowl, combine egg, milk, and butter; add flour mixture and blend until smooth. Pour over apples. Sprinkle with remaining ¼ cup nuts. Bake for 50 minutes. Serve with whipped topping or whipped cream sprinkled with cinnamon if desired.

Lois Rhodes
Harrisonburg, VA

Magic Cobbler

½ cup butter
¾ cup milk
2 cups sugar, divided
1 cup flour
1½ teaspoons baking powder
2 cups fruit (peaches, apples, blueberries, blackberries, etc.)

Preheat oven to 350°. In 8x11-inch pan, melt butter. In mixing bowl, combine milk, 1 cup sugar, flour, and baking powder. Pour mixture over melted butter, but do not stir. Spread fruit on top and sprinkle with remaining 1 cup sugar. Again, do not stir. Bake for 30 to 40 minutes or until fruit is soft.

Rosanna Helmuth
Arthur, IL

Mom's layin' over the dough—she's got to get her bakin' caught after.

Apple Goodie

5 to 6 apples, peeled and sliced
¾ teaspoon cinnamon
½ cup sugar
I cup quick oats
¾ cup brown sugar
½ cup flour
⅛ teaspoon salt
⅓ cup butter

Preheat oven to 350°. Spread apples in 9-inch square baking dish.
Sprinkle with mixture of cinnamon and sugar. Mix oats, brown sugar,
flour, salt, and butter until crumbly; sprinkle on top of apples. Bake for
35 minutes or until apples are soft. Serve warm with milk or ice cream.

Sarah Schwartz
Marlette, MI

Pumpkin Rolls

3 eggs

I cup sugar

⅔ cup pumpkin

I teaspoon lemon juice

¾ cup flour

I teaspoon baking powder

2 teaspoons cinnamon

I teaspoon ginger

½ teaspoon nutmeg

½ teaspoon salt

Preheat oven to 375°. Beat eggs in mixing bowl on high speed for 5 minutes. Beat in sugar. Stir in pumpkin and lemon juice. Combine dry ingredients and fold into pumpkin mixture. Spread into greased and floured 10x15-inch pan. Bake for 15 minutes. Remove cake from oven and turn onto clean linen towel dusted with powdered sugar. Roll towel and cake together. Cool. Unroll cooled cake; spread with filling and roll back up.

Filling

I cup powdered sugar

¼ cup butter, softened

6 ounces cream cheese

I teaspoon vanilla

Blend filling ingredients until smooth.

Elizabeth Borntrager
Brown City, MI

Banana Split Dessert

3 cups graham cracker crumbs
½ cup margarine, melted
1 (8 ounce) package cream cheese, softened
1½ cups powdered sugar
1 teaspoon vanilla
1 (20 ounce) can crushed pineapple, drained
3 bananas, sliced
1 (16 ounce) carton frozen whipped topping, thawed
Chocolate syrup

Preheat oven to 350°. Combine graham cracker crumbs and melted margarine. Press mixture into 9x13-inch baking pan and bake for 5 minutes. Cool. Mix cream cheese, powdered sugar, and vanilla. Spread over crust. Spread pineapple on top of cream cheese; arrange bananas on top of pineapple. Top with whipped topping and drizzle with chocolate syrup. Refrigerate.

Carolyn Wenger
Elk Horn, KY

Rhubarb Dessert

4 cups chopped rhubarb
1 cup sugar
1 (4 ounce) package strawberry gelatin
1 cake mix (white or yellow)
2 cups water

Preheat oven to 350°. Layer ingredients in 9x13-inch baking pan. Do not stir. Bake for 40 minutes.

Janet Martin
Ephrata, PA

◆ ◆ ◆

Seeing ourselves as others see us will not do us much good, for we will not believe what we see.

◆ ◆ ◆

Rhubarb Torte

CRUST

1½ cups flour

2 tablespoons sugar

Pinch of salt

½ cup butter

Preheat oven to 325°. Mix crust ingredients until crumbly and press into 8x10-inch baking pan. Bake for 20 to 25 minutes.

FILLING

2¼ cups chopped rhubarb

1½ cups sugar

2 to 3 cups whole milk

2 to 4 tablespoons flour

3 egg yolks

1 teaspoon vanilla

Combine filling ingredients in saucepan and cook until thick. Pour over crust.

TOPPING

3 egg whites

¼ teaspoon cream of tartar

6 tablespoons sugar

Preheat oven to 350°. Beat topping ingredients until stiff. Spread over filling. Brown in oven for 10 to 15 minutes.

Mrs. Bruce Troyer
Crab Orchard, KY

Apple Pandowdy

FILLING

4 cups peeled and sliced apples

1 cup brown sugar

¼ cup flour

½ teaspoon salt

1 tablespoon vinegar

¾ cup water

1 tablespoon butter

1 teaspoon vanilla

Preheat oven to 400°. Spread apples in bottom of 9x13-inch baking pan. To make syrup, combine sugar, flour, salt, vinegar, and water in saucepan. Bring to a boil and cook for 2 minutes. Remove from heat and add butter and vanilla. Pour over apples.

TOPPING

1 cup flour

½ teaspoon salt

2 teaspoons baking powder

2½ tablespoons shortening

½ cup milk

Mix flour, salt, baking powder, and shortening with pastry cutter. Add milk and stir just until moistened. Drop by spoonfuls over apple filling. Bake for 35 minutes. Serve with whole milk or cream. Yields 6 to 8 servings.

Marie Zimmerman
Pembroke, KY

Blueberry Dessert

1½ cups graham cracker crumbs
½ cup butter or margarine, melted
1 (8 ounce) package cream cheese, softened
2 eggs
1 cup sugar
1 (21 ounce) can blueberry pie filling
Whipped topping (optional)

Preheat oven to 350°. Combine graham cracker crumbs and melted butter. Press into 8x11-inch glass baking dish. Mix cream cheese, eggs, and sugar until smooth and pour over crumb layer. Bake for 20 minutes or until brown around the edges. Cool. Spread pie filling over cream cheese layer. Top with whipped topping if desired. Yields 6 to 8 servings.

Mrs. Paul Schrock
Marion, MI

● ● ◆

*A good temperature is
a cool head and
a warm heart.*

◆ ● ◆

Raisin Mumbles

FILLING

2½ cups raisins

½ cup sugar

2 tablespoons cornstarch

1 cup water

3 tablespoons lemon juice

Preheat oven to 350°. Cook all ingredients in saucepan, stirring constantly on low heat until thick (about 5 minutes). Set aside to cool while preparing crumb mixture.

CRUMB MIXTURE

¼ cup butter

1 cup brown sugar

½ teaspoon baking soda

1½ cups quick oats

Scant 1¾ cups flour

Cream butter and sugar. Add dry ingredients and mix well. Press half the crumb mixture into 9x13-inch pan. Spread filling on top; sprinkle with remaining crumbs. Bake for 25 to 30 minutes.

Lydia Hoover
Denver, PA

Amish and Mennonite Quilts

Both Old Order Amish and Mennonite women have a great appreciation for flowers, gardens, and quilts. A quilt shows love much the same as a favorite food that is carefully prepared as a display of affection. Quilt patterns are a reflection of daily living and often resemble things found in nature. A quilt displays a woman's ability as a seamstress, and she may show her quilts for the admiration of others without intimidation. Her quilts reflect her personality, as does a well-kept home or garden.

At a very young age, Amish and Mennonite girls are taught the basics of sewing quilt patches. Quilting techniques are passed from generation to generation, and quilts are often passed down to children and grandchildren. Many Amish and Mennonite women find time to quilt during long winter evenings. It's a relaxing pastime that is also very worthwhile. Often women will get together for an all-day quilting bee, which is also a time of fellowship.

There are many different quilt shapes and patterns. Among them are Diamond in Square, Bars, Log Cabin, Double Wedding Ring, Dahlia, Lone Star, Fan, Tumbling Block, Distelfink, Grandmother's Choice, and many others.

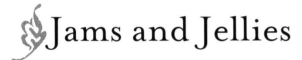# Jams and Jellies

*The first of the firstfruits of thy land thou shalt bring
into the house of the LORD thy God.*

EXODUS 23:19

Peach
Marmalade

5 cups mashed peaches
7 cups sugar
2 cups crushed pineapple
1 (6 ounce) package gelatin (peach, apricot, orange,
or raspberry)

Combine peaches, sugar, and pineapple in saucepan. Boil for 15 minutes. Add gelatin and stir until dissolved. Pour into containers. Cool; freeze or seal.

Linda Fisher
Leola, PA

♦ ♦ ♦

Laughter is the jam on the toast of life; it adds flavor, keeps it from becoming too dry, and makes it easier to swallo

♦ ♦ ♦

Strawberry Rhubarb Jam

5 cups diced rhubarb
4 cups chopped strawberries
5 cups sugar
2 (6 ounce) packages strawberry gelatin

Combine rhubarb and strawberries in 6-quart kettle and boil for 10 minutes. Add sugar and boil 10 minutes longer, stirring constantly. Add gelatin and stir until dissolved. Pour into jars and seal.

Lena Miller
Apple Creek, OH

Yellow Pear
Tomato Preserves

5 cups yellow pear tomatoes
6 cups sugar
1 (3 ounce) package lemon gelatin
1 (3 ounce) package apricot gelatin

Wash tomatoes and cut into halves; place in saucepan. Add sugar and bring to a hard boil for 15 minutes. Add gelatin and stir until dissolved. Pour into jars and seal.

Sharri Noblett
Port Arthur, TX

♦ ♦ ♦

Blessed is the close-knit family whose bonds of love extend to eac one in the home and to eac and every friend.

♦ ♦ ♦

Zucchini Apricot Jam

6 cups peeled and shredded zucchini
6 cups sugar
¾ cup crushed pineapple, undrained
½ cup lemon juice
1 (6 ounce) package apricot gelatin

Place zucchini and sugar in large, heavy saucepan. Cook on low heat until sugar is dissolved. Bring to a boil and cook for 15 minutes. Add pineapple with juice and lemon juice and boil for 6 minutes. Remove from heat; add gelatin and stir until dissolved. Pour into jars and seal. Yields 5 pints.

Rachel Stutzman
Dalton, OH

Baked Apple Butter

7 pounds apples or 4 quarts applesauce
2 tablespoons cinnamon
6 cups brown sugar
½ cup vinegar or cider
1 cup crushed pineapple, drained

Preheat oven to 350°. When using apples, cook until soft, cool, and put through sieve. Add cinnamon, sugar, vinegar, and pineapple to applesauce and mix well. Pour into baking dish, cover, and bake for 3 hours, stirring occasionally. Pour into jars and seal. Note: Recipe may be tripled to make a large batch and will fit into a 13-quart stainless steel bowl.

Mrs. Daniel Gingerich
Rensselaer Falls, NY

Red Beet Jelly

6 cups beet juice (use same day or juice will darken)
2 packages Sure-Jell
½ cup lemon juice
8 cups sugar
1 (6 ounce) package raspberry gelatin

Combine juice, Sure-Jell, and lemon juice in saucepan and bring to a boil. Add sugar all at once and heat to boiling. Boil for 5 minutes. Remove from heat. Add gelatin and stir until dissolved. Pour into jars and seal.

Clara Miller
Fredericktown, OH

If we don't plant knowledge when we are young, it will give us no shade when we are old.

Cantaloupe Preserves

2 pounds firm, ripe cantaloupe
4 cups sugar
Juice of 1 lemon
1 (3 ounce) package gelatin (peach, apricot, or
    orange)

Pare cantaloupe and cut into thin slices, 1 inch long. Combine cantaloupe slices and sugar and let set overnight. Add lemon juice and cook
until clear. Add gelatin and stir until dissolved. Pour into jars and seal.
Yields 2 pints.

Rebecca Stauffer
Elk Horn, KY

*Happiness is like jam;
you can't spread even a
little without getting
some of it on yourself.*

Grape
Butter

4 cups grapes, crushed
4 cups sugar

Combine grapes and sugar and let set overnight. Place in saucepan and cook for 20 minutes; put through sieve. Bring mixture back to a boil. Pour into jars and seal.

Mrs. Levi Gingerich
Dalton, OH

Amish Homes

Most Amish have large families and large homes. The absence of electrical lines and the presence of a long clothesline indicates an Amish home in Plain communities. Amish houses are simple, and ornamentation is kept to a minimum. A cupboard filled with fancy dishes is permissible in many communities, and so are some paintings and calendars, but photographs of people are not permissible. Many Amish kitchens have finely made cabinets and hot and cold running water. Pumps to circulate water are often operated with compressed air, and water heaters often use propane gas. Conventional refrigerators and stoves also operate on propane. Some Amish still use wood-burning stoves, especially during the cold winter months.

Since there are no electric lights in an Amish home, kerosene- or gasoline-burning lamps are used. Space heaters that burn wood, coal, kerosene, or propane are often used for heating. Old-fashioned hand pumps are still used in some of the more traditional homes, but many Amish homes now have a modern tap that brings drinking water to the kitchen from the well. Amish who have pressurized or gravity-flow water systems can have modern plumbing without electric pumps. More than half of all Amish homes are now equipped in this way. In some communities bottled gas is used to heat water, but in some of the more conservative groups, only wood, coal, or kerosene water heaters are allowed.

Linoleum floors are typical, and wall-to-wall carpets are rare. In some Amish communities, dark green shades are used to cover the windows, and in other places simple curtains are used. A typical Amish home will have a living room, kitchen, parents' bedroom, and bathroom on the main floor. The second floor will include several more bedrooms, and there is often a basement used for laundry and storage below the first floor.

Main Dishes

She riseth also while it is yet night,
and giveth meat to her household,
and a portion to her maidens.

<small>PROVERBS 31:15</small>

Zucchini Casserole

1 large zucchini, shredded

1 onion, chopped

3 raw potatoes, shredded

2 cups sausage or hamburger

Salt and pepper to taste

1 cup shredded cheddar cheese

2 to 3 tomatoes, sliced

Preheat oven to 350°. Combine all ingredients except tomatoes and spread in greased baking dish. Arrange tomatoes on top. Bake for 1 hour.

Elva Shirk
Dundee, NY

Hamburger Cabbage Casserole

1 pound hamburger
1 small onion, chopped
6 cups shredded cabbage
1 (14.5 oz.) can tomato soup, diluted with 1 can water

Preheat oven to 350°. Brown hamburger with onion. Grease baking dish and place shredded cabbage on bottom. Add hamburger and onions. Pour diluted tomato soup on top. Bake for 1 hour or until cabbage is tender.

Mary Alice Kulp
Narvon, PA

> ◆ ◆ ◆
>
> *When a man does the dishes, it's called helping; when a woman does the dishes, it's called life.*
>
> ◆ ◆ ◆

Laura's Casserole

2 cups cooked chicken, cut in small pieces

2 cups uncooked macaroni or noodles

2 cans cream of chicken soup

2 cups milk

½ cup chopped onion

¼ teaspoon black pepper

3 tablespoons butter

1 cup shredded cheese

Preheat oven to 350°. Layer ingredients in large baking dish in order given and bake for 30 to 40 minutes or until done.

Laura Schwartz
Stanwood, MI

The secret of success in conversation is to be able to disagree without being disagreeable.

Dairy
Casserole

8 cups shredded raw potatoes

2 cups uncooked macaroni

2 cups fresh, frozen, or canned peas

2 cups cooked meat (ham, sausage, etc.)

3 teaspoons salt

½ cup chopped onion

4 cups shredded cheese

2 quarts milk

Preheat oven to 325°. Layer ingredients in large baking dish in order given and pour milk over all. Bake for 2½ hours. Yields 15 servings.

Ruth Martin
Selinsgrove, PA

Stuffed Pepper Casserole

2 pounds hamburger, browned
1½ cups chopped cabbage
1 large tomato, peeled and chopped
2 large yellow tomatoes, peeled and chopped
1¼ cups uncooked minute rice
1 medium onion, chopped
4 peppers, red and green, chopped
2½ cups water
1 tablespoon salt
1 teaspoon pepper
1 cup shredded cheddar cheese

Preheat oven to 375°. Combine all ingredients except cheese. Pour into baking dish with lid. Top with shredded cheese. Bake, covered, for 1½ hours or until rice is tender. Note: This is a low-fat food.

Lucy Zimmerman
Orrstown, PA

Wisconsin Caserole

5 raw potatoes, shredded

2 cups uncooked macaroni

2 cups fresh, frozen, or canned peas or corn

2 cups cooked meat (ham, sausage, etc.)

3 teaspoons salt

½ cup shredded onion

2 cups shredded cheese

2 quarts milk

Preheat oven to 350°. Combine all ingredients in baking dish. Bake at 350° for 2 hours or at 300° for 3 hours or until done.

Mrs. Mervin Hoover
Curtiss, WI

The bridges you cross before you come to them are over rivers that aren't there.

Pot Roast with Mushroom Gravy

1 (3½ pound) boneless beef roast
2 large garlic cloves, thinly sliced
1 teaspoon salt
1 teaspoon garlic salt
1 teaspoon pepper
¼ cup flour
3 tablespoons vegetable oil
2 cups brewed coffee
1 can cream of mushroom soup
1 tablespoon Worcestershire sauce
1 large onion, sliced
3 tablespoons cornstarch
3 tablespoons water

Cut slits in roast with a sharp knife. Push a garlic slice into each slit. Sprinkle roast with salts and pepper. Lightly dredge in flour, patting off excess flour. Brown roast on all sides in hot oil in large Dutch oven. Blend coffee, soup, and Worcestershire sauce and pour over roast; top with onions. Cover and simmer for 3 hours or until tender. Reserve drippings to make gravy. Combine cornstarch and water. Stir into drippings. Bring mixture to a boil and cook for 1 minute or until thickened. Pour gravy over roast.

Barbara Miller
Camden Wyoming, DE

Baked Pork Chops

Pork chops
Salt
Hickory smoke salt
Barbecue seasoning
Worcestershire sauce
Lemon juice
Parsley flakes

Preheat oven to 350°. Sprinkle each pork chop with salt, hickory smoke salt, and barbecue seasoning on both sides. Lay flat in baking pan and pour 1 teaspoon Worcestershire sauce and 1 teaspoon lemon juice over each pork chop. Sprinkle with parsley flakes. Bake at 350° for 50 minutes and then at 400° for 20 minutes.

Susie Martin
Penn Yan, NY

> ♦ ♦ ♦
>
> *May everyone who shares my table see the love of God living in and through me.*
>
> ♦ ♦ ♦

Scalloped Potatoes
and Pork Chops

5 cups peeled and thinly
   sliced raw potatoes
1 cup chopped onion
Salt and pepper to taste
1 can cream of mushroom soup
½ cup sour cream
6 pork loin chops (1 inch thick)
Chopped fresh parsley

Preheat oven to 375°. In greased 9x13-inch baking pan, layer half the potatoes and onion and sprinkle with salt and pepper. Repeat layer. Combine soup and sour cream and pour over potato mixture. Cover and bake for 30 minutes. Meanwhile, in skillet, brown pork chops on both sides. Place pork chops on top of casserole. Cover and return to oven for 45 minutes or until pork chops are tender. Uncover during last 15 minutes of baking. Sprinkle with parsley. Yields 6 servings.

Mrs. Enos Christner
Bryant, IN

Yummasette

1 large package egg noodles
3 pounds ground beef
1 onion, chopped
2 cans cream of mushroom soup
1 can cream of chicken or celery soup
1 cup sour cream
2 cups fresh, frozen, or canned peas
½ loaf buttered, toasted bread crumbs

Preheat oven to 350°. Cook noodles in salt water until done. Cook ground beef and onion in butter until done. In large bowl, combine soups, sour cream, peas, noodles, beef and onion, and half the bread crumbs; mix well. Pour into greased baking dish, top with remaining bread crumbs, and bake for 1 hour.

Edna and Lois Hoover
Mifflinburg, PA

A gracious word may smooth the way; a joyous word will light the day; a peaceful word will lessen stress; a loving word will heal and bless.

Sweet and Sour
Meatballs

3 pounds hamburger

1 cup chopped onion

Salt and pepper to taste

1 cup milk

2 cups quick oats

Preheat oven to 350°. Mix meatball ingredients and shape mixture into balls. Combine sauce ingredients. Place meatballs in shallow baking pan and pour sauce over them. Bake for 30 to 40 minutes.

Sauce

1 cup ketchup

½ cup vinegar

2 tablespoons Worcestershire sauce

2 tablespoons brown sugar

Emma Eicher
Geneva, IN

Potato Sausage Pie

3 teaspoons vegetable oil
3 cups shredded raw potatoes
1 cup shredded cheese
¾ cup sausage
¼ cup chopped onion
1 cup milk
2 eggs
½ teaspoon salt
⅛ teaspoon pepper

Preheat oven to 425°. Combine oil and potatoes. Press into pie pan. Bake for 15 minutes or until crust begins to brown. Remove from oven and layer potatoes with cheese, sausage, and onion. Combine milk, eggs, salt, and pepper and pour over layered ingredients. Bake 30 minutes longer or until lightly browned. Cool for 5 minutes before cutting.

Annie Stauffer
Elk Horn, KY

You must forgive someone their faults or you will never get close enough to admire their goodness.

Chicken Pie

2 cups chicken broth
2 tablespoons flour
2 cups diced cooked potatoes
2 cups diced cooked carrots
2 cups cooked peas
2 tablespoons chopped cooked celery
1 small onion, chopped and cooked
2 cups diced cooked chicken
Buttered bread crumbs or pie dough rolled out to
  fit oblong baking pan

Preheat oven to 350°. Heat broth. Add 2 tablespoons flour to make a thin gravy. Mix with vegetables and chicken. Pour into oblong baking pan and cover with bread crumbs or pie dough. Bake for 1 hour.

Rebekah Mast
Amelia, VA

The highest reward for a person's toil is not what they get for it, but what they become by it.

Golden Baked Chicken

6 chicken breasts, cut up
½ cup flour
½ teaspoon salt
Dash of pepper
½ teaspoon paprika
¼ cup butter, melted
1 can cream of chicken soup
¼ cup water
1 tablespoon minced parsley

Preheat oven to 375°. Coat chicken with mixture of flour, salt, pepper, and paprika. Arrange chicken in a single layer in buttered shallow baking dish. Drizzle melted butter over chicken. Bake for 20 minutes. Turn chicken over and bake 20 minutes longer. Mix cream of chicken soup with ¼ cup water and pour over chicken. Sprinkle with parsley. Bake an additional 20 minutes.

Edna Nisley
Baltic, OH

Chicken Dumplings

2 cups chopped mixed vegetables (potatoes, carrots,
   celery, and onions)
1 cup chopped chicken
Water
Salt and chicken flavoring to taste

Cook vegetables until soft. Place chicken in 3-quart saucepan and cover
with water; add salt and chicken flavoring. Heat to boiling and cook until
chicken is done. Add vegetables and bring back to a boil before adding
dumpling dough.

DUMPLINGS

1½ cups flour
⅓ cup butter, softened
1 teaspoon salt
2 teaspoons baking powder
2 teaspoons sugar
Milk

Combine flour, butter, salt, baking powder, and sugar. Add enough
milk to make a stiff dough. Drop by spoonfuls in boiling chicken mixture. Cover and reduce heat for 20 minutes without lifting lid.

Ada Miller
Norwalk, WI

German Pizza

1 pound ground beef
½ medium onion, chopped
½ green pepper, diced
1½ teaspoons salt, divided
½ teaspoon pepper
2 tablespoons butter
6 raw potatoes, shredded
3 eggs, beaten
⅓ cup milk
2 cups shredded cheddar or mozzarella cheese

In 12-inch skillet, brown beef with onion, green pepper, ½ teaspoon salt, and pepper. Remove beef mixture from skillet; drain skillet and melt butter. Spread potatoes over butter and sprinkle with remaining 1 teaspoon salt. Top with beef mixture. Combine eggs and milk and pour over all. Cook, covered, on medium heat until potatoes are tender, about 30 minutes. Top with cheese; cover and heat until cheese is melted, about 5 minutes. Cut into wedges or squares to serve. Yields 4 to 6 servings.

Mrs. Danny Miller
Lakeview, MI

Lazy Wife's Dinner

1 cup diced raw potatoes
1 cup diced carrots
1 cup cooked meat
1 cup uncooked macaroni
3 tablespoons chopped onion
1 can cream of chicken, mushroom, or celery soup
1½ cups frozen vegetables
1½ cups milk
1 cup shredded cheese

Preheat oven to 350°. Combine all ingredients and pour into baking dish. Bake, covered, for 1½ hours.

Susie Blank
Narvon, PA

A hungry man need not be pressed to be a willing table guest.

Chicken and Filling

1 chicken, boiled or baked and deboned
8 to 10 cups bread cubes
2 medium onions, chopped
½ cup shredded carrots or chopped sweet peppers
½ cup diced celery (optional)
1 teaspoon salt
1 teaspoon pepper
2 teaspoons paprika
1 cup chicken broth

Preheat oven to 300°. Combine all ingredients and pour into baking dish. Bake for 1 hour. Serve with gravy.

Lisa Martin
Shippensburg, PA

Chicken Chowder

2 tablespoons butter
¼ cup chopped onion
1½ cups cubed cooked chicken
1½ cups diced carrots
1½ cups diced raw potatoes
2 chicken bouillon cubes
1 teaspoon salt
⅛ teaspoon pepper
2 cups water
3 tablespoons flour
2½ cups milk

Melt butter in 3-quart saucepan. Add onions and sauté until tender.
Add chicken, carrots, potatoes, bouillon cubes, salt, pepper, and water.
Cover and simmer until vegetables are tender. Combine flour and ½
cup milk in a jar. Shake until blended. Add to vegetables along with
remaining 2 cups milk. Cook on medium heat, stirring constantly, until
mixture thickens. Yields 1¾ quarts.

Ella Miller
Fresno, OH

♦ ♦ ♦

*Help my words be graciou
and tender today, for
tomorrow I may have
to eat them.*

♦ ♦ ♦

Cheddar Chowder Soup

2 cups water
2 cups peeled and diced raw potatoes
½ cup diced carrots
½ cup diced celery
¼ cup chopped onions
1 teaspoon salt
¼ teaspoon pepper

WHITE SAUCE
¼ cup butter
¼ cup flour
3 cups milk
2 cups shredded cheddar cheese
1 cup cubed ham

Combine water, potatoes, carrots, celery, onion, salt, and pepper in large kettle. Boil for 10 to 12 minutes. Meanwhile, to make white sauce, melt butter in saucepan; add flour and stir until smooth. Slowly add milk and cook until thickened. Add cheese and stir until melted. Add ham to undrained vegetables. Combine sauce with vegetables and ham and heat through. Serve with crackers.

Mrs. Delbert Schrock
Whitehall, MT

Good Ham Soup

1 cup carrots, sliced
½ cup celery, sliced
1 cup diced raw potatoes
¼ cup minced onion
2 teaspoons chicken base
1½ cups diced ham
¼ cup butter or margarine
⅓ cup flour
1 quart milk
1½ cups shredded American cheese

Combine vegetables in large kettle and cover with water. Add chicken base and cook until tender. Add ham. To make sauce, melt butter in saucepan; add flour and stir until smooth. Slowly add milk and cook until thickened. Combine sauce with vegetables and ham. Add cheese and heat until melted.

Annamae Auker
Elk Horn, KY

Potato Soup

⅓ cup diced carrots
⅓ cup diced celery
¼ cup diced onion
2 tablespoons butter
2 tablespoons flour
1 quart milk
2 chicken bouillon cubes
2 tablespoons fresh parsley
½ teaspoon salt
½ teaspoon seasoned salt
¼ teaspoon cayenne pepper
6 potatoes, cooked

Sauté carrots, celery, and onion in butter. Add flour and stir until smooth. Slowly add milk and cook until thickened. Add bouillon cubes, parsley, salt, seasoned salt, and cayenne pepper. Simmer for 20 minutes. Cube half the potatoes and mash the other half; add all to soup. Simmer until heated through.

Mrs. Reuben Yoder
Quaker City, OH

One today is worth two tomorrows.

Split Pea
Soup

½ pound green or yellow split peas

4 cups water

1 ham hock or meaty ham bone

⅓ cup diced carrots

⅓ cup diced celery

⅓ cup diced onion

½ teaspoon salt

Wash and drain split peas. Combine all ingredients in kettle with tight-fitting lid. Bring to a boil. Reduce heat and simmer, covered, for 2 hours, stirring occasionally. Remove ham hock or bone. Cool slightly. Cut meat off bone and dice. Add to soup and heat thoroughly. Note: Split peas do not require soaking.

Sarah Troyer
Mercer, PA

Amish Bean Soup

2 to 3 tablespoons butter
3 quarts milk (approximately)
Salt to taste
8 cups stale homemade bread cubes
I cup cooked navy beans (optional)

Brown butter in saucepan; add milk and bring almost to a boil. Add salt and enough bread to thicken. Cover and let set for 10 minutes before serving. Add beans if desired.

Lucy Hackman
Mansfield, OH

◆ ◆ ◆

Whistle and hoe, sing as you go; shorten the row by the songs you know.

◆ ◆ ◆

Hearty Chicken 'n' Rice Soup

1½ cups chicken broth
3 cups cold water
½ cups uncooked rice
½ cup diced carrots
½ cup diced celery
¾ pound processed cheese, cubed
1½ cups diced cooked chicken

In saucepan, combine broth, water, rice, carrots, and celery and bring to a boil. Cover and simmer for 25 minutes. Add cheese and chicken; stir until cheese is melted.

Judith Martin
Millmont, PA

Rivel
Soup

2 cups flour
½ teaspoon salt
1 egg, well beaten
1½ to 2 quarts chicken or beef broth
1 can corn, crushed

Combine flour, salt, and beaten egg and mix with fingers until mixture is crumbly. Heat broth; add corn and bring back to a simmer. Drop rivels slowly into broth. Cook for about 10 minutes. Rivels will look like boiled rice when cooked. Note: Chopped carrots, celery, and onion may be added if desired.

Esther Stauffer
Port Trevorton, PA

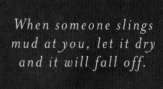

When someone slings mud at you, let it dry and it will fall off.

Cheeseburger Soup

2 pounds ground beef
¾ cup chopped onion
1 quart chicken broth
2 cups water
4½ cups diced raw potatoes
1½ cups shredded carrots
1½ cups diced celery
1½ teaspoons salt
¾ teaspoon pepper

WHITE SAUCE
½ cup butter
¾ cup flour
3 cups milk
3 cups processed cheese, cubed

Brown ground beef with onion; drain. In large saucepan, combine broth, water, vegetables, salt, and pepper. Bring to a boil. Cook for 5 to 10 minutes or until potatoes are tender. To make white sauce, melt butter in saucepan; add flour and stir until smooth. Slowly add milk and cook until thickened. Add cheese and stir until melted. Combine sauce with vegetables and ground beef and onion. Do not boil after sauce is added to vegetables.

Esther Coblentz
Fredericksburg, OH

Taste of Home Tomato Soup

1 cup chopped celery
1 cup chopped onion
1 carrot, shredded
1 small green pepper, chopped
¼ cup butter or margarine
4½ cups chicken broth, divided
4 cups peeled and chopped tomatoes
2 teaspoons sugar
½ teaspoon curry powder
½ teaspoon salt
¼ teaspoon pepper
½ cup flour

In 3-quart saucepan, cook celery, onion, carrot, and green pepper in butter until tender. Add 4 cups broth, tomatoes, sugar, curry powder, salt, and pepper. Bring to a boil. Reduce heat; simmer, uncovered, for 20 minutes. In small bowl, stir flour and remaining ½ cup broth until smooth. Gradually stir into tomato mixture. Bring to a boil. Cook and stir until thick and bubbly, about 2 minutes.

Nancy Ann Stoltzfus
Gap, PA

Buttery Onion Soup

2 cups thinly sliced onions
½ cup butter
¼ cup flour
2 cups chicken broth
2 cups milk
1½ cups processed cheese, shredded
Salt and pepper to taste
Parsley flakes (optional)

In large kettle, sauté onions and butter on low heat until tender, about 15 minutes. Blend in flour and add broth and milk. Cook and stir on medium heat until bubbly. Cook and stir for 1 minute. Reduce heat to low; add cheese and stir until melted. Add salt and pepper. Garnish with parsley flakes and serve. Yields 1½ quarts (6 servings).

Miriam Yoder
Houstonia, MO

◆ ◆ ◆

Dig your neighbor out of trouble, and you'll find a place to bury yours.

◆ ◆ ◆

Creamy Broccoli Soup

¾ cup peeled and cubed raw potatoes
1 medium carrot, sliced
2 cups chopped broccoli
2 tablespoons butter
2 tablespoons flour
1½ cups milk
½ teaspoon salt
Dash of nutmeg
Dash of pepper

Cook potatoes and carrots in small saucepan; drain and set aside. Cook broccoli in separate saucepan; drain and set aside. Melt butter in saucepan; add flour and stir until smooth. Slowly add milk. Bring to a boil until thickened. Add salt, nutmeg, and pepper. Then add potatoes, carrots, and broccoli.

Susie Beachy
McIntire, IA

Amish and Mennonite Transportation

Old Order Amish and many Old Order Mennonites use a horse and buggy for their everyday transportation. They believe that owning a car is in direct opposition to the values of nonconformity, simplicity, humility, and self-denial. Also, cars usually have radios and air conditioners and require insurance to drive, all of which is prohibited by the conservative Plain People's church rules.

Many people believe that since the Amish don't own cars, they don't ride in them and oppose all modes of public transportation. This notion isn't true, as the Amish and Old Order Mennonites will hire English drivers to take them places they can't go with their horse and buggy. When traveling long distances, the Amish and Mennonites use public transportation, such as buses, trains, and ships. However, air travel is considered to be too worldly by most of the Old Order groups, except in extreme emergencies.

Each Amish community has a distinct style of horse-drawn vehicle. Those in some communities are completely black, while others are gray, like those in Lancaster County, Pennsylvania. Some buggies have yellow or white tops, such as the ones driven by the Amish in an area west of Harrisburg, Pennsylvania, known as "Big Valley."

The more modern Mennonites drive cars. The cars of more conservative modern Mennonites are usually black and quite plain, while the cars of those among the most liberal group of Mennonites are as modern as the cars driven by the English.

Miscellaneous

A merry heart doeth good like a medicine:
but a broken spirit drieth the bones.

PROVERBS 17:22

Plant
Food

1 gallon tepid water
1 teaspoon Epsom salts

Combine water and Epsom salts and use to water your plants. Use 1 quart
tepid water instead of 1 gallon for tomatoes suffering from blight.

Mary J. Miller
Medford, WI

Stainless Steel Cleaner

18 quarts very warm water
½ cup lye
1 cup Clorox bleach
1 cup detergent (any kind)

Dissolve lye in water. Add bleach and detergent and mix well. Soak pots and pans for 5 minutes or so in this solution, removing plastic handles if possible. Dip aluminum cake pans for just a minute. Also use on Tupperware, Corelle, silverware, utensils, and burners. Solution can be kept for a few days if your cleaning is not done. No matter how dirty the solution is, it will still clean. Pour solution down the drain when finished.

Mrs. Mose Slabaugh
Spikard, MO

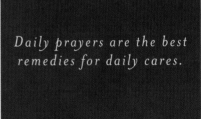

Daily prayers are the best remedies for daily cares.

Window
Cleaner

1 pint (2 cups) rubbing alcohol
½ cup ammonia
1 teaspoon liquid dish soap

Combine all ingredients. Pour into 1-gallon jug and fill with water. Fill a spray bottle to use.

Mary Raber
Holmesville, OH

Peanut Butter Suet
for Birds

1 cup crunchy peanut butter
1 cup lard
2 cups quick oats
⅓ cup sugar
1 cup wheat flour
2 cups cornmeal
1 cup wild bird feed

Melt peanut butter and lard together. Stir in remaining ingredients.
Press into cake pan. Allow to cool, then cut into squares. Store in freezer
or cool place.

Miriam Miller
Stanford, KY

> *Them that works hard,
> eats hearty.*

Nonstick Cooking Spray

Liquid lecithin
Olive oil

Mix equal parts liquid lecithin and olive oil. Brush into your cookware and bakeware for nonstick cooking. Very little is needed. Note: Liquid lecithin can be purchased at most health food stores and some bulk food stores.

Miriam Miller
Stanford, KY

When the outlook is not good, try the up look.

Homemade Play Dough

2 cups flour
½ cup cornstarch
1 tablespoon powdered alum
1 cup salt
1 tablespoon vegetable oil
4 tablespoons cream of tartar
2 cups boiling water

In large bowl, combine flour, cornstarch, alum, salt, oil, and cream of tartar. Add boiling water and stir until mixed. Knead with hands. May add food coloring or divide into portions and add different colors. Cool and store in tightly covered jars. Play dough will last a long time if children are taught to cover it when not in use.

Ada Miller
Norwalk, WI

Homemade Cough Syrup

Honey
Lemon juice

Mix equal parts honey and lemon juice and stir well. Store in refrigerator. Note: Cough syrup will separate quickly.

Anna Hershberger
Fredericksburg, OH

The Great Physician always has the right remedy.

Kidney Stone Remedy

6 red beets
3 quarts water

Clean and wash beets (don't peel or slice). Combine beets and 3 quarts water in kettle. Boil slowly so as not to boil the water away. After 1 hour, strain the water into a jar and store in a cool place so remedy won't sour. Drink 3 glasses a day until gone. Almost never is a second dose necessary. The kidney stones don't pass; they just melt away.

Ida Miller
Medford, WI

Remedy for Upset Stomach

2 cups water
¼ teaspoon baking soda
2 tablespoons honey or sugar
¼ cup orange juice

Mix all ingredients in blender. Take 1 tablespoon every half hour or as tolerated. Take right away after vomiting if possible.

Mrs. John Beachy
Mount Victory, OH

Varicose Vein Salve

1 pound lard
2 heaping handfuls marigold flower heads and
    leaves, chopped up

Heat lard until it crackles. Remove from heat and add chopped-up marigolds. Do not boil. Stir well. Cover and let stand overnight. Heat again and put through strainer or old cloth. Pour into jars and store in a cool place. Put on legs as needed.

Annie Peachey
Letart, WV

◆ ◆ ◆

*It is not where we are
but who we are that creates
our happiness.*

◆ ◆ ◆

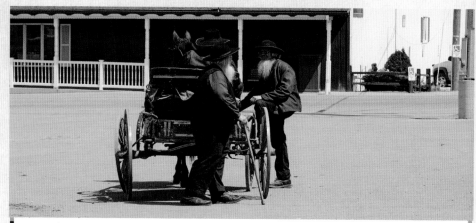

Amish Communication

Amish communication has undergone many changes in the last several years. While the Amish still rely on letters and word of mouth, many of them now have telephones available to use for their businesses, to call for a ride from an English driver, to let out-of-town relatives know of a death in the family, or for emergency purposes. Some Amish use pay phones or go to a neighbor who isn't Amish to use the phone, while others have telephones outside their homes in sheds, barns, or places of business. Many Amish with phones have answering machines or voice messaging. In a number of Amish communities, several Amish families might share a phone in a centrally located shed.

Since the Amish rely heavily on mail as a means of communication, the arrival of mail each day is an important event. Personal as well as business transactions are made via mail by the Amish, and some Amish participate in circle letters, which allow people of similar interests or occupations to correspond with each other.

The Amish also use newspapers and magazines to communicate, using want ads or informative letters from church members in various communities. A newspaper called *The Budget* includes such letters from Amish, Mennonite, and other Plain groups. There are other periodicals for the Plain People as well, including a montly magazine called *The Connection.*

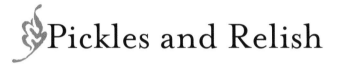# Pickles and Relish

*If ye have faith as a grain of mustard seed,
ye shall say unto this mountain, Remove hence to yonder place;
and it shall remove; and nothing shall be impossible unto you.*

MATTHEW 17:20

Bread and Butter Pickles

25 medium cucumbers
10 medium onions
½ cup salt
1 cup water
2 cups sugar
2 teaspoons celery seed
2 teaspoons mustard seed
1½ teaspoons turmeric
1 cup vinegar

Slice cucumbers and onions. Add salt and let stand a few hours. Drain. Add water, sugar, spices, and vinegar. Pour into jars and seal. Process in hot water bath for 15 minutes.

Anna Yoder
Marlette, MI

A pint of example is worth barrel full of advice.

Sweet
Dills

Cucumbers, sliced
Fresh dill heads
Garlic cloves

Fill jars with sliced cucumbers, adding 2 bunches of dill and 3 or 4 garlic cloves to each quart. Pour brine over cucumbers.

BRINE

1 quart weakened vinegar (½ water may be used)
2 cups water
¼ cup salt
4 cups sugar

Bring all brine ingredients to a boil. Immediately fill jars and put on lids. Process jars in hot water bath for about 10 minutes.

Susanna M. Schrock
Wheatland, MO

Quick Dill Pickles

Fresh dill heads (or dill seed)
1 garlic clove per jar
¼ teaspoon powdered alum per jar
Cucumbers, whole or sliced
1 quart vinegar
3 quarts water
1 cup canning salt

Put 1 dill head, 1 garlic clove, and alum in each quart jar. Then pack cucumbers in jars. Combine vinegar, water, and salt; fill up jars as needed and put on lids. Set jars in hot water bath and bring water to a boil; remove jars. Variation: Add heaping ¼ cup sugar to brine.

Ada Troyer
Mercer, PA

If you trust, you don't worry; if you worry, you don't trust.

Salad Dressing
Pickles

12 large cucumbers
½ cup salt
3 quarts water
12 onions
3 cups sugar
½ cup flour
1 tablespoon celery seed
1 tablespoon turmeric
½ teaspoon red pepper (scant)
2 sweet peppers (optional)
1 pint (2 cups) vinegar
1 pint (2 cups) water

Peel and slice cucumbers and let stand overnight in brine made with ½ cup salt and 3 quarts water. Drain off salt water. Slice onions thinly and combine with cucumbers, sugar, flour, spices, vinegar, and water in large kettle. Bring to a boil. Pack into jars while hot and seal.

Mary Miller
Medford, WI

Pickled Corn

2 pints (4 cups) vinegar
1 cup sugar
1 tablespoon salt
8 cups fresh corn (about 12 ears)
½ head cabbage, finely chopped
2 ripe peppers, finely chopped
1 tablespoon celery seed
1 tablespoon mustard seed

In large kettle, combine vinegar, sugar, salt, and corn; bring to a boil. Add cabbage, peppers, celery seed, and mustard seed; bring to a boil again and cook a little longer. Pour into jars and seal.

Lydia Schwartz
New Auburn, WI

Pickled Beets

3 quarts cooked beets
3 cups cider vinegar
I cup water
4 cups sugar
3 teaspoons salt
3 teaspoons pickling spice

Peel cooked beets and cut up. Combine vinegar, water, sugar, salt, and pickling spice; heat mixture and add to beets. Pour into jars and seal. Process jars in hot water bath for 5 minutes.

Savannah Troyer
Atlantic, PA

A long face and a broad mind are rarely found under the same hat.

Green Tomato Relish

18 green tomatoes, quartered
8 red peppers, quartered
4 green peppers, quartered
6 onions, quartered
3 cups vinegar
3 cups sugar
1 tablespoon celery seed
1 cup water
1½ tablespoon salt
4 tablespoons prepared mustard

Grind tomatoes, peppers, and onions; drain well. Add vinegar, sugar, celery seed, water, and salt to ground mixture. Pour into saucepan and cook for 15 minutes. Combine mustard with a little water or milk and add to cooked mixture. Cook 2 minutes longer. Pour into jars and seal. Use like ketchup.

Annetta Martin
New Holland, PA

Corn
Relish

6 pints fresh sweet corn
4 peppers (any color), chopped
3 onions, chopped
1 bunch celery, chopped
2 cups sugar
2 cups vinegar
2 tablespoons salt
1 teaspoon mustard seed
2 cups water

Combine all ingredients in saucepan and cook until tender. Pour into jars and seal. Process jars in hot water bath for 10 minutes.

Lucy Zimmerman
Orrstown, PA

Our deeds speak so loudly that our words can't be heard.

Zucchini
Relish

12 cups ground zucchini
4 cups ground onion
1½ cups ground red and green peppers
2 tablespoons salt
2½ cups vinegar
6 cups sugar
1 tablespoon dry mustard
1½ teaspoons celery seed
¾ teaspoon turmeric
¼ teaspoon pepper
¾ teaspoon cornstarch

Grind zucchini, onion, and peppers with salt. Let stand overnight.
Rinse with cold water and drain in colander. In large kettle, mix vinegar,
sugar, mustard, celery seed, turmeric, pepper, and cornstarch; cook until mixture begins to thicken. Add zucchini mixture and mix well. Cook
for 30 minutes. Pour into hot, sterilized jars and seal.

Barbara Stutzman
Apple Creek, OH

Over-100-Year-Old Apple Relish

16 cups cored and ground apples
8 cups ground onions
2 cups hot red peppers (jalapeño or other)
8 cups vinegar
12 cups sugar

Core and grind apples. Grind onions and peppers. Combine all ingredients and cook in large kettle until mixture thickens. Simmer for 45 minutes to 1 hour, stirring constantly. If mixture becomes dry, add a little more vinegar. Skim off foam. Pour into sterilized jars and seal.

Sharri Noblett
Port Arthur, TX

Eat an apple, save the core; plant the seeds and raise some more.

Amish Occupations

When the Amish first came to America, most of the men farmed for a living. Now the price of land is at a premium, and large tracts of land are difficult to find. Many Amish men now work at various trades, including dairy farming, livestock raising, carpentry, blacksmithing, harness making, and several others.

Some young Amish women have jobs in businesses, where they must use telephones and computers, but the typical single Amish woman works as a cook or waitress in a restaurant, does part-time cleaning for non-Amish neighbors, works in a bakery or cheese shop, or teaches in one of the local one-room schoolhouses. In some Amish communities, married women work out of their homes. Some have opened their homes to serve meals to groups of tourists. Others sell eggs, baked goods, quilts, or various handmade items from their home or nearby business. A few married women have part-time jobs outside the home, cooking in restaurants or tending market stands several days a week.

Amish children are taught at an early age to help with family chores, and by the time they have graduated from the eighth grade, the boys are ready to learn a trade or help their fathers farm the land, while the girls prepare for marriage and learn how to run a household. Amish children often tend small roadside stands on their property, where they sell produce, baked goods, and crafts to tourists and their non-Amish neighbors.

Salads and Sides

Now he that planteth and he that watereth are one: and every man
shall receive his own reward according to his own labour.

1 CORINTHIANS 3:8

German Potato Salad

4 boiled potatoes, cut in chunks
1 teaspoon sugar
½ teaspoon salt
¼ teaspoon dry mustard
Dash of pepper
2 tablespoons vinegar
1 cup sour cream
½ cup thinly sliced cucumbers or onions
2 to 3 slices bacon, fried and cut into small pieces
Paprika

Combine sugar, salt, dry mustard, pepper, vinegar, sour cream, cucumber or onion, and bacon pieces. Pour over warm potatoes and toss lightly until coated with dressing. Serve warm with a dash of paprika.

Ruth Martin
Selinsgrove, PA

One who works in a garden works hand in hand with God.

Cauliflower-Broccoli Salad

1 bunch broccoli, cut in bite-size pieces
1 head cauliflower, cut in bite-size pieces
8 slices bacon, fried and crumbled
⅓ cup chopped onion
1 cup shredded cheese

DRESSING
1 cup mayonnaise
⅓ cup sugar
2 tablespoons vinegar

In large bowl, combine broccoli, cauliflower, bacon, onion, and cheese; set aside. In separate bowl, combine dressing ingredients and stir until smooth. Just before serving, pour dressing over salad and toss to coat. Yields 6 to 8 servings.

Kara Martin
Shippensburg, PA

Sweet Potato Salad

2 pounds sweet potatoes
1½ cups mayonnaise
2 teaspoons Dijon mustard
¼ teaspoon salt
4 hard-cooked eggs, chopped
1½ cups finely chopped celery
8 green onions, sliced

Place sweet potatoes in large saucepan and cover with water. Cover and cook gently until potatoes can be easily pierced with the tip of a sharp knife. Drain. When potatoes are cool, peel and dice. In large bowl, combine mayonnaise, Dijon mustard, and salt. Stir in eggs, celery, and onions. Add potatoes and toss gently to coat. Cover and refrigerate for 2 to 4 hours. Yields 8 to 10 servings.

Lydia Hoover
Denver, PA

Winter Fruit Salad

1 (20 ounce) can pineapple chunks, undrained
1 (3 ounce) package vanilla cook-and-serve pudding
    mix
4 cups mixed fresh fruit chunks (apples, bananas,
oranges, pears, etc.)
¾ cup chopped pecans or walnuts
⅓ cup flaked coconut
Whipped topping (optional)

Drain pineapple, reserving juice. Set pineapple aside. In saucepan, combine pineapple juice and pudding mix. Cook on medium heat until thickened. Cool. In large bowl, combine pineapple, other fruit chunks, nuts, and coconut. Add dressing and toss to coat. Refrigerate until ready to serve. Garnish with whipped topping if desired.

Norma Zimmerman
Latham, MO

♦ ♦ ♦

*Disappointments are
like weeds in the garden;
you can let them grow and
take over your life, or you
can rout them out and let
the flowers sprout.*

♦ ♦ ♦

Banana Pineapple Salad

1 (20 ounce) can crushed pineapple, undrained
2 (3 ounce) packages lemon gelatin
4 cups hot water
16 large marshmallows
4 bananas, sliced
1 cup pineapple juice
½ cup sugar
2 tablespoons flour
2 tablespoons butter
2 eggs, beaten
1 cup frozen whipped topping, thawed
Crushed nuts

Drain pineapple, reserving juice. Dissolve gelatin in hot water. Stir in marshmallows until melted. Cool. Add bananas and drained pineapple. Spread in 9x13-inch pan and refrigerate until firm. Cook pineapple juice, sugar, flour, butter, and eggs until thick, stirring constantly. Cool. Fold in whipped topping. Spread mixture over salad. Sprinkle with crushed nuts. Refrigerate until ready to serve. Yields 12 servings.

Magdalena Stutzman
Sullivan, IL

Amish Broccoli Salad

4 bunches broccoli, cut in bite-size pieces (8 cups)
1 jar bacon bits
1 large red onion, chopped
⅓ cup raisins (optional)
1 cup mayonnaise
¼ cup sugar
2 tablespoons cider vinegar
½ teaspoon pepper
½ cup sunflower seeds, toasted

In large bowl, combine broccoli, bacon bits, onion, and raisins. In small bowl, blend mayonnaise, sugar, vinegar, and pepper and pour over broccoli mixture. Toss to coat. Refrigerate for 2 hours. Just before serving, add sunflower seeds.

Marianne Schmucker
Greenville, PA

Every time you turn green with envy, you are ripe for trouble.

Sauerkraut
Salad

4 cups sauerkraut
1 cup sugar
1 cup shredded carrots
1 cup chopped celery
½ cup chopped onion (or less)

In medium bowl, combine sauerkraut and sugar. Let set for 8 hours.
Add carrots, celery, and onion to sauerkraut mixture and mix well.

Alice Stauffer
Leonardtown, MD

*The things we grow used to
are the things we love best,
the ones we are certain have
weathered the test.*

Dutch Slaw

1 large head cabbage, chopped
1 cup diced celery
1 green pepper, diced
½ cup chopped onion
½ cup vinegar
2 cups sugar
2 teaspoons salt
½ teaspoon mustard seed
1 teaspoon celery seed

Combine all ingredients, place in glass jar, and screw on lid. Slaw is ready to serve. May be kept in an icebox a long time.

Ruth Martin
Selinsgrove, PA

Yummy Macaroni Salad

1 pound macaroni
1 cup chopped green pepper
4 carrots, shredded
1 cup chopped onion
1 (14 ounce) can sweetened condensed milk
1 cup sugar
1 cup vinegar
2 cups mayonnaise
Salt and pepper to taste

Cook macaroni; drain and cool. Add remaining ingredients and toss lightly. Chill for several hours. Best if refrigerated overnight.

Mary Lynn Weaver
Jamestown, PA

Sour Bean Salad

1 can yellow or baby lima beans, drained
1 can kidney beans, drained
1 can green beans, drained
½ cup chopped onion
½ cup chopped green pepper
¾ cup sugar
½ cup vinegar
1 tablespoon vegetable oil

Combine drained beans, onion, and pepper. In saucepan, combine vinegar, sugar, and oil; heat until sugar is dissolved. Add to bean mixture. Refrigerate overnight to blend flavors.

Mrs. Eddie Raber
Holmesville, OH

♦ ♦ ♦

If we don't cut the peace pattern right, we will have scraps.

♦ ♦ ♦

Grandma Auker's Cranberry Salad

4 oranges, peeled
4 apples
1 cup water
1 (6 ounce) package strawberry or raspberry gelatin
2 (16 ounce) cans cranberry sauce
1 (8 ounce) can crushed pineapple, drained

Grind oranges and apples; set aside. In saucepan, bring 1 cup water to a boil. Remove from stove and add gelatin; stir until dissolved. Add cranberry sauce and stir. Then add pineapple and ground apples and oranges. Pour into bowl and chill to set.

Annamae Auker
Elk Horn, KY

The Lord often digs wells of joy with the spade of sorrow

Good Red
Beets

4 cups sugar

2 cups vinegar

1 quart beet juice (from kettle of cooked beets)

1 tablespoon salt

2 teaspoons cinnamon or mixed pickling spice

3 quarts of small cooked beets

Combine first five ingredients in kettle and bring to a boil. Add to cooked beets.

Fannie Stutzman
Dalton, OH

Sweet and Sour Green Beans

4 slices bacon
½ cup chopped onion
2 tablespoons flour
¾ cup water
⅓ cup cider vinegar
2 tablespoons sugar
6 to 8 cups cooked green beans, drained

In skillet, cook bacon until crisp. Drain, reserving 2 tablespoons drippings. Crumble bacon and set aside. Sauté onions in drippings until tender. Add flour and stir until smooth. Add vinegar and sugar. Cook and stir until thick and bubbly. Cook and stir 2 minutes longer. Gently stir in beans and heat through. Sprinkle with bacon. Serve immediately. Yields 6 to 8 servings.

Jeanette Leinbach
Cumberland, PA

*One business policy that nev
needs changing is honesty.*

Scalloped Cabbage

1 large head cabbage
3 tablespoons butter
3 tablespoons flour
1 can cream of mushroom soup
¼ cup milk
2 tablespoons chopped onion
2 tablespoons chopped green pepper
1½ teaspoons Worcestershire sauce

Cook cabbage in a little water until tender; drain. Meanwhile, melt butter in saucepan; add flour and stir until smooth. Add soup, milk, onion, green pepper, and Worcestershire sauce and cook on medium heat until onions and peppers are soft and sauce is smooth and thick. Add cabbage and heat through.

Ida Miller
Smicksburg, PA

Creamy Mashed Potatoes

12 large potatoes, peeled and cooked
1 (8 ounce) package cream cheese
1 cup sour cream
2 teaspoons salt
½ teaspoon garlic salt
½ cup margarine

Preheat oven to 350°. Mash potatoes. Add cream cheese, sour cream, salt, garlic salt, and margarine; blend well. Spoon into baking dish and bake for 1 hour. Mashed potatoes can be frozen until ready to use.

Martha Yoder
Crofton, KY

If you listen to too much advice, you may wind up making other people's mistakes.

Baked Beans

2 pounds dry Great Northern beans

1 pound bacon

4 cups tomato juice

1 cup brown sugar

1 cup sugar

1 teaspoon dry mustard

1 medium onion, chopped

2 teaspoons Worcestershire sauce

Salt and pepper to taste

Sort beans and soak overnight. The next morning, preheat oven to 350°. Drain beans; cover with water and cook until soft. Cut bacon into small pieces and fry. Add bacon, drippings, tomato juice, sugars, mustard, onion, Worcestershire sauce, salt, and pepper to cooked beans. Pour into baking dish and bake for 1 hour.

Thelma Zook
Oakland, MD

Baked Sweet
Corn

4 cups sweet corn (fresh, frozen, or canned)
3 eggs, beaten
2 tablespoons cornstarch
1½ cups milk

Preheat oven to 350°. Combine corn, eggs, cornstarch, and milk and bake, uncovered, for 1 hour. Cook topping ingredients in a kettle until clear and pour over baked corn; continue to bake until set.

TOPPING
½ cup butter
½ cup water
½ cup sugar
1 tablespoons cornstarch

Sarah Troyer
Mercer, PA

Sweet Potatoes

Sweet potatoes
Butter, melted
Crushed cornflakes
Salt and pepper to taste

Preheat oven to 350°. Peel and slice sweet potatoes. Dip slices in melted butter and coat with crushed cornflakes. Sprinkle with salt and pepper. Place on cookie sheet. Bake for 35 to 45 minutes or until done.

Anna Beechy
Topeka, IN

◆ ◆ ◆

The best way for a woman to have a few minutes to herself is to start doing the dishes.

◆ ◆ ◆

Onion
Rings

4 medium onions, sliced (any thickness)
¾ cup flour
1 egg, beaten
⅔ cup milk
1 teaspoon salt
1 teaspoon vegetable oil

Soak onion slices in cold water for 1 hour or longer. Combine flour, egg, milk, salt, and oil; mix well. Dip onion slices in batter and deep fry until golden brown.

Kathryn Louise Stoltzfus
Paradise, PA

There is one thing you will be sure to have help in doing, and that's minding your own business.

Zucchini and Cheese

1½ pounds zucchini, sliced ¼-inch thick
2 medium tomatoes, sliced
¼ cup flour
1½ teaspoons salt, divided
¼ teaspoon pepper, divided
1½ teaspoon oregano, divided
¼ cup vegetable oil
1 cup sour cream
½ cup grated Parmesan cheese

Preheat oven to 350°. Combine flour, ½ teaspoon salt, ⅛ teaspoon pepper, and ½ teaspoon oregano. Toss zucchini slices in flour mixture and brown in oil for 4 minutes on each side. Spread into greased 8-inch square baking dish. Top with tomato slices. Mix together remaining 1 teaspoon salt, ⅛ teaspoon pepper, 1 teaspoon oregano, and sour cream. Spread on top of tomato slices. Top with Parmesan cheese. Bake for 30 to 35 minutes.

Mrs. Ervin Miller
Clark, MO

German-Style Green Beans

6 slices bacon

1 large onion

4 cups green beans

1 tablespoon cornstarch

¼ teaspoon dry mustard

2 tablespoons brown sugar

1 tablespoon vinegar

Cut bacon into small pieces and fry. Dice onion and fry in bacon grease. Set aside. Drain green beans, reserving 1 cup liquid; dissolve cornstarch in bean liquid. Add dry mustard, brown sugar, and vinegar and cook in saucepan until thickened. Add green beans, bacon, and onion and simmer until hot.

Beverly Stauffer
Elk Horn, KY

Amish Dressing

6 eggs

4 cups milk

1½ cups chicken broth

Salt and pepper to taste

½ teaspoon seasoned salt

½ teaspoon celery salt (optional)

1 loaf bread, cubed and toasted

2 cups diced cooked potatoes

½ cup diced cooked carrots

½ cup chopped celery

4 cups diced cooked chicken

½ cup butter, melted and browned

Beat eggs, milk, and broth; add seasonings. Pour over bread cubes. Add vegetables, chicken, and browned butter; mix well. Let set for 30 minutes to allow bread to absorb liquid. Fry in large skillet with additional butter until browned. Turn over frequently while frying, but do not stir.

Sue Miller
Strasburg, PA

Thanksgiving Filling Balls

1 loaf bread, cubed
1 medium onion, diced
3 stalks celery, diced
1 cup butter, melted
1 teaspoon salt
½ teaspoon pepper
2 tablespoons parsley flakes
1½ cups milk
2 eggs
1½ cups mashed potatoes

Preheat oven to 350°. Combine all ingredients and shape into balls.
Bake in greased baking dish, covered, for 1 hour. If necessary, add a little
water to bottom of dish to keep balls from drying out.

Carolyn Brubaker
Port Trevorton, PA

Amish and Mennonite Clothes

For most Plain People, style of dress is a minor issue in their total belief system, but they do feel it is important to wear nonconforming clothing. They believe modest, simple dress is essential to their Christian discipleship, and the practice of wearing plain clothes is based on a number of scriptures and scriptural principles, such as is found in Romans 12:2: "And be not conformed to this world: but be ye transformed by the renewing of your mind, that ye may prove what is that good, and acceptable, and perfect, will of God."

The Amish feel that all their clothing should be made of only solid-colored fabrics. Mennonite women, however, often use patterned fabrics, which some say do not show dirt as easily. The more conservative groups specify that the figures and patterns in the material must be small. For church, most Old Order Amish and Mennonite women wear capes, triangular forms worn over the top of their dresses. Aprons that cover the fronts of their dresses are also worn most of the time. Both conservative Amish and Mennonite women wear *kapps* (head coverings), and when they go out in public, they wear larger black bonnets over the *kapps*. Around home, some young Amish women and children wear scarves on their heads.

Old Order Amish and Mennonite men and boys wear broad-brimmed hats—straw hats for warmer weather and black wool or felt hats for colder weather or dress. Stocking caps are also worn during the colder months. The width of the brim and hat band, as well as the height and shape of the crown, varies among church groups. For everyday work, they wear plain dark pants held up by suspenders. They also wear solid-colored shirts. For church, the men wear dark slacks and jackets.

# Snacks

The meek shall eat and be satisfied:
they shall praise the LORD that seek him:
your heart shall live for ever.
PSALM 22:26

Auntie Anne's Soft Pretzels

1¼ cups lukewarm water
1 tablespoon yeast
¼ cup brown sugar
2 cups flour
2 cups bread flour
1 cup cold water
1 tablespoon baking soda
Pretzel salt
Onion powder (optional)
Butter, melted

Preheat oven to 475°. In large bowl, stir together warm water, yeast, and brown sugar. Add both flours to yeast mixture. Mix well and let rise for 20 minutes. To form pretzels, first combine water and baking soda. Then cut dough in pieces and roll into ropes. Dip in baking soda solution and place on a towel to drain for a few minutes. Transfer to greased cookie sheets. Sprinkle with pretzel salt and onion powder if desired. Bake for 12 minutes or until golden brown. Dip in melted butter before serving.

Melinda Kanagy
Belleville, PA

Honey Mustard Pretzels

2 pounds hard sourdough pretzels

1 cup vegetable oil

1½ cups prepared mustard

½ cup honey

¼ cup onion powder

Preheat oven to 200°. Break pretzels as finely as possible into large bowl. In separate bowl, combine oil, mustard, honey, and onion powder. Pour over broken pretzels and mix thoroughly with spatula, making sure every pretzel is coated. Spread in large baking or roasting pan and bake for 2 hours, stirring every 15 to 20 minutes. Store in airtight container.

Melissa Martin
Trenton, KY

Soda Crackers

4 cups flour
1 teaspoon baking powder
¾ cup lard
½ cup brown sugar
1 egg, beaten
Milk
Seasonings (poultry seasoning, onion powder,
  cloves, etc.)

Preheat oven to 375°. Mix together flour, baking powder, lard, brown
sugar, and egg. Add enough milk to make a wet dough. Roll out dough
on floured board as thinly as possible. Sprinkle with poultry seasoning
(or any seasoning of your choice). Cut into squares with cutter. Prick
with fork. Bake on heated cookie sheet for 10 minutes or until lightly
brown and hard. Note: If cookie sheet is not heated before adding
dough, crackers will stick to pan.

Carolyn Kline
Shreve, OH

◆ ◆ ◆

*One thorn of experience is
worth more than a wilderness
of advice or warning.*

◆ ◆ ◆

Amish Peanut Butter Spread

2 cups brown sugar
1 cup water
1 teaspoon maple extract
2 cups peanut butter
1 (16 ounce) jar marshmallow crème

In saucepan, combine brown sugar, water, and maple extract and bring to a boil. Blend peanut butter and marshmallow crème. Then blend both mixtures together until smooth. Serve as a spread on bread or crackers.

Saloma Stutzman
Navarre, OH

Cinnamon Popcorn

13 quarts freshly popped corn
1 cup sugar
1 cup cinnamon imperials
½ cup light corn syrup
1 teaspoon salt
1 cup margarine
1 teaspoon vanilla
½ teaspoon baking soda

Preheat oven to 250°. In heavy saucepan, combine sugar, cinnamon imperials, light corn syrup, salt, and margarine; boil for 5 minutes. Add vanilla and baking soda; mix well. Pour over popped corn and mix well. Place in large roasting pan or on two cookie sheets and bake for 1 hour, stirring every 10 to 15 minutes.

Sarah Miller
Fredonia, PA

♦ ♦ ♦

If you have not often felt the joy of doing a kindly act, you have neglected much, and mostly yourself.

♦ ♦ ♦

Great Granola Bars

5 cups quick oats

4½ cups crispy rice cereal

1 cup flaked coconut

1 package graham crackers, crushed

¾ cup butter

¼ cup vegetable oil

¼ cup honey

¼ cup peanut butter

2 (10½ ounce) packages miniature marshmallows

2 cups semisweet chocolate chips

In mixing bowl, combine oats, crispy rice cereal, coconut, and crushed graham crackers. Melt butter in saucepan and add oil, honey, peanut butter, and marshmallows. Stir on low heat until marshmallows are melted. Pour over dry ingredients and mix well. Stir in chocolate chips. Press granola onto large cookie sheet. Cut into bars and enjoy. Yields 3 dozen bars. Note: Do not bake.

Edna Troyer
Baltic, OH

Fruit Roll-ups

2 (3 ounce) packages gelatin (any flavor)
1 cup boiling water
3 cups miniature marshmallows

Combine all ingredients in saucepan. Heat and stir until marshmallows
are melted. Pour into 9x13-inch baking pan or small cookie sheet with
sides. When firm, cut into strips and roll up.

Nancy Burkholder
Bergholz, OH

Caramel Apple Dip

½ cup butter
1 cup sugar
½ cup light corn syrup
1 (14 ounce) can sweetened condensed milk

Combine butter, sugar, and light corn syrup in saucepan. Cook on
medium heat until butter is melted. Add sweetened condensed milk and
boil for 3 minutes. Serve warm with apple wedges.

Verna Weaver
Withee, WI

Cheese Ball

2 (8 ounce) packages cream cheese
½ teaspoon garlic salt
1½ teaspoons parsley flakes
1½ teaspoons onion flakes
1½ teaspoons Accent seasoning
2 (3 ounce) jars chipped dried beef
Crushed nuts or graham cracker crumbs

Mix all ingredients except nuts or crumbs and shape into ball. Roll in crushed nuts or graham cracker crumbs.

Rose Marie Shetler
Berne, IN

Crunchy Swiss and Ham Appetizers

2 cups very stiff mashed potatoes
2 cups cooked ham, finely chopped
1 cup shredded Swiss cheese
⅓ cup mayonnaise
¼ cup minced onion
1 egg, well beaten
1 teaspoon prepared mustard
½ teaspoon salt
¼ teaspoon pepper
3½ cups crushed cornflakes

Preheat oven to 350°. Combine all ingredients except cornflakes; chill. Shape into 1-inch balls and roll in cornflakes. Place on greased cookie sheet and bake for 25 to 30 minutes. Serve hot. Yields about 8 dozen appetizers.

Elizabeth Shrock
Jamestown, PA

Index